Bismillah

Fofky's Kitchen: Easy Ivorian Recipes for Traditional and Street Foods

By

Papatia Feauxzar

DJARABI KITABS PUBLISHING

Dallas, Texas

Fofky's Kitchen

For information contact:
Djarabi Kitabs Publishing
P.O. BOX 703733
Dallas, TX 75370
USA
www.djarabikitabs.com

Cover design by Sam Rog
Interior design by Papatia Feauxzar
Recipes' pictures by Fofky's Team
Pictures by Pixabay: Café, Sandwiches, Tapioca Pudding, Lemon Grass Leaves, Daisy's Tea, Rice Porridge, Sirups, Yoghurt and Skewers
Pictures by Unsplash: Oatmeal Porridge and Fruit Salad
Pictures by Yasmine - Journal d'une Foodie aka Afrofoodie : Crab,-Fish-Snail Stew and Plantain Patties

Paperback ISBN-13: 978-1-947148-15-4
Paperback ISBN-10: 1-947148-15-X

Library of Congress Control Number: 2018949553
First Print Edition: September 2018

10 9 8 7 6 5 4 3 2 1

Contents

Foreword

Peace and Blessings! When we first came to the United States of America as students in the early 2000s, the first thing we missed from Ivory Coast was food. At the time, Ivorian Cuisine wasn't easily accessible in America. Most of the time, we ate cafeteria food at the university. The strange dishes with the unfamiliar tastes gave us our first taste of culture shock, but we had no choice but to get used to the food or starve.

Cultural Food is an identity card. It brings people together and lifts spirits in times of lows. However, without our daily cultural background (Ivorian Cuisine), nostalgia hit us; and hard. In time, we became independent and started finding our way around town to make our favorite Ivorian dishes and each bite took us down a delicious memory lane. We had made it a point to find our relatives living in the city near to our school so we could at least visit and relish Ivorian Cuisine with them once in a blue moon.

Today, Ivorian Cuisine has started to gain recognition across the globe. In addition, many Millennium and post-Millennium Ivorians are seeking restaurants to enjoy their favorite traditional dishes and street foods. Others simply want to know how to cook the same dishes their ancestors made. This cookbook is an easy to follow guide to help anyone curious about what Ivorian Cuisine is.

Enjoy, break bread, visit family and memories with each bite ...and don't forget to please leave a review.

H. bint Youssef
Gbâkêla—Chef
Fofky's Kitchen
Food & Beverages

Part 1: What is Ivorian Cuisine?

Ivorian Cuisine comes from Ivory Coast; a country located on the West Coast of Africa with beautiful beaches and resorts bordering the Atlantic Ocean. Formerly known as the **Republic of Côte d'Ivoire**, it is located between Ghana and Liberia at the South. Liberia, Mali and Burkina Faso are its neighboring countries toward the north. A former French colony, the national language remains French. Before France, Portugal was there, hence the similarities between many Latin American countries' and Ivorian cuisine. To continue, the political and administrative capital is Yamoussoukro. The name is after a former queen of the city named **Yamoussou**. In Baoulé, a sub-ethnic group of the Akan group, *kro* means town.

The motto of this prosperous and small country (322,643 km^2) is **Union-Discipline-Travail**. In English, it means **Unity-Discipline-Work**. The anthem of Ivory Coast is *L'Abidjannaise*. The land was void of any inhabitants until all the ethnic groups migrated from the countries surrounding Ivory Coast to converge and settle there. They lived in peace until greed, power and politics turned them against each other and sat the country back for years. All praises to God, the peace has returned. And we pray it lasts.

Some known Ivorians include al-Azhar graduate and former bank director **Imam Aboubacar Fofana**, Jeddah, Makkah and Washington D.C. graduate **Imam Cissé Djiguiba**, Son Excellence Monsieur le Président **Allassane Dramane Ouattara**, Award-Winning Musician **Aïcha Koné**, Soccer players **Didier Drogba** and the **Touré Brothers**, Taekwondo gold medalist **Cheick Sallah Cissé** and Sprinter silver medalist **Murielle Ahouré**.

To cut the history lesson short, much like French Cuisine, **Ivorian Cuisine** is as diverse as the four main ethnic groups of the country and the sixty plus languages of its inhabitants. Akans, Mandés, Gours, and Krous all contribute to the diversity and plethora of the Ivorian Cuisine and pride of the continent. Moreover, the fact that Ivory Coast is the number one producer of cocoa in the world and also ranks in the top category as a coffee producer adds to this justified pride. In this cookbook, we will try to give you recipes for as many dishes and drinks as we can.

Dansé or Akwaba—Welcome and have a seat! It will be worth the ride.

Part 2: The Recipes

BREAKFASTS

"My favorite Ivorian breakfast is Gbinzin because it reminds me of the holidays in the country side with my great aunt. They were fun times."— Fasi Diallo

GBINZIN OR BOUILLIE DE MAÏS CASSÉ-CASSÉ

Cornmeal Porridge

(Serves 4)

YOU WILL NEED

- 2 cups of fine to coarse cornmeal
- 1 cup of sugar
- 4 - 8 cups of water
- ½ a lemon
- Milk (optional)

PROCEDURE

- Boil the water.
- Add the washed cormeal to it.
- Stir occasionally and cook to al-dente or 20 mins.
- Add sugar, lemon, and let it simmer for 5 - 10 mins
- Serve and eat. Add milk if needed.

TOP INSIGHT

Gbinzin is a highly nutritious, delicious and rich dish taste wise. It can be consumed anytime during the day but it's preferable to eat it in the morning or at night after dinner.

BOUILLIE DE BANANE MÛRES

Plantain Banana Porridge

(Serves 4)

YOU WILL NEED

- 3 Banane Mûres (Ripe Plantain Bananas)
- 2 tablespoons of peanut butter
- 2 tablespoons of palm oil nut
- ¼ - ½ cup of sugar
- A pinch of salt
- ½ a teaspoon of cayenne pepper (optional)
- 5 - 6 cups of water

PROCEDURE

- Peel the plantain bananas and dice them. Next, put them in a pot.
- Add peanut butter, water, oil and salt.
- Then, bring them to boil. It should take about 10 to 15 minutes.
- Once soft and cooked, use a hand blender to blend them directly from the cooking pot. The one used in Ivory Coast is a wooden spatula with a cross at the tip. The cook rubs the handle of the utensil between hand palms until the mixture is blended.
- Add sugar, pepper. Cook for 5 - 10 mins. Then, serve and eat.
- Refrigerate any remainder. This is valid for any perishable dish in this cookbook.

TOP INSIGHT

This porridge is nutty, sweet and creamy. Try out the recipe and enjoy the food bliss.

MALO BACCA OR BOUILLIE DE RIZ

Rice Porridge

(Serves 3-4)

YOU WILL NEED

- 1 cup of long or round grain rice
- 4 cups of water
- 1 - 2 cups of sugar
- 1 small rock of *potasse* salt (edible potash) or 1/4 teaspoon of baking soda.
- 1 tablespoon of olive oil
- 1 cup of liquid milk (optional)
- A pinch of salt if no potasse available (optional) and Sucre Vanillé (optional)
- Powdered or condensed milk (optional)
- Plain yoghurt (optional)

PROCEDURE

- Wash the rice and bring it to boil. Add the potasse and the oil. Tip*: Potasse helps food cook faster and gives the porridge a special taste. It's available in African groceries stores. After 15 - 20 mins of cooking, add liquid milk, and sugars.
- Cook for another 5 - 10 mins. Grains of rice should be really soft and look like a porridge. When time elapses, serve and eat. It can be served hot or cold. In our opinion, hot Bacca is for breakfast and cold Bacca is for dessert. Your choice! You can also season your Bacca to your liking with yoghurt, powdered or condensed milk.

TOP INSIGHT

Malo Bacca or Brâh Gbê (white porridge) is the ultimate breakfast for rural Ivorians and others who don't mind eating it in the city. Often served with milk or plain yoghurt made from fresh cow's milk, it will keep you full for many hours; perhaps until lunch time. Malo (Rice in Mandé) Bacca also has a highly spiritual and religious aspect. It's often used for *saraqah (sadaqah)* events. It's the preferred dish of choice for these religious charity events.

KABBA BACCA OR BOUILLIE DE MAÏS

Corn Porridge

(Serves 2-3)

YOU WILL NEED

- 2/3 of a cup of granulated corn
- 3 cups of water
- 1 lemon
- 1 - 2 cups of sugar
- 1 smashed root of ginger or 1 tsp of cayenne pepper (optional)

PROCEDURE

- Put the water in a pot and let it boil. In the meantime, juice the lemon and add the baobab powder to it.
- Mix them well. If thick, you can add more water to your liking to make it lighter. Now, add some water to the ginger paste and filter the juice out.
- Mix the ginger juice to the lemon and baobab fusion. Back to the pot, when the water boils, add half the grains, stir, and let them boil for five minutes. Stir so that the grains don't stick together or to the bottom of the pot.
- After five minutes, add the other half of the grains, stir, and let the contents of the pot boil. You can divide the grains in several lots. It's up to you. When the grains are soft and cooked, add the lemon/baobab/ginger juices to the pot.
- Let it boil for a few minutes before adding the sugar and it's ready.

TOP INSIGHT

Bacca de Maïs is a porridge made out of yellow corn couscous. Kabba is corn in Mandingue. The grains are made from yellow corn powder. To save you the hassle of making them yourself, these grains are available to purchase at African groceries stores. If you can't find them, find the YouTube video of **Cuisine, Trucs et Astuces de Binta** in order to make them from scratch.

GNOMI BACCA OR BOUILLIE DE MIL

Millet Porridge

(Serves 2-3)

YOU WILL NEED

- 2/3 of a cup of granulated millet
- 3 cups of water
- 1 lemon
- 1 - 2 cups of sugar
- 2 to 3 Tbsps. of baobab powder (optional)
- 1 smashed root of ginger or 1 tsp of cayenne pepper (optional)

PROCEDURE

- Put the water in a pot and let it boil. In the meantime, juice the lemon and add the baobab powder to it.
- Mix them well. If thick, you can add more water to your liking to make it lighter. Now, add some water to the ginger paste and filter the juice out.
- Mix the ginger juice to the lemon and baobab fusion. Back to the pot, when the water boils, add half the grains, stir, and let them boil for five minutes. Stir so that the grains don't stick together or to the bottom of the pot.
- After five minutes, add the other half of the grains, stir, and let the contents of the pot boil. You can divide the grains in several lots. It's up to you. When the grains are soft and cooked, add the lemon/baobab/ginger juices to the pot.
- Let it boil for a few minutes before adding the sugar and it's ready.

TOP INSIGHT

Gnomi Bacca or millet porridge is mostly the dish that draws many non-Muslims to Mandingue Muslim homes during Ramadan. They love it just as much as African Muslims do! We have a tradition to gift Gnomi Bacca to our neighbors and relatives during this blessed month. And non-Muslims patiently await the month so that they can taste this dish again. Though, we cooked it in our homes outside of Ramadan for breakfast or the fasting days scattered around the *hijri* calendar several times a year, it is a dish very special to Ramadan in West Africa. It's made the same way as the previous recipe; Bacca de Maïs. Millet is gluten free.

BOUILLIE DE FONIO

Fonio Porridge

(Serves 2-3)

YOU WILL NEED

- 1 cup of fonio
- 4 cups of water
- 1 -2 cups of sugar
- 1 cup of liquid milk (optional)
- Powdered or condensed milk (optional)
- Plain yoghurt

PROCEDURE

- Wash the grains and bring them to boil.
- After 15 - 20 mins of cooking, add liquid milk, and sugars.
- Cook for another 5-10 mins. Grains of fonio should be really soft and look like a porridge.
- When time elapses, serve and eat.
- You can also season your porridge to liking with yoghurt, powdered or condensed milk.

RIZ COUCHÉ

Overnight Stew and Rice

(Serves 1-2)

YOU WILL NEED

- Rice from the previous day (s)
- Stew from the previous day (s)
- Spices (Optional)

TOP INSIGHT

Riz Couché is simply a meal from the previous day or days that is warmed up. It's eaten when the mixture is hot enough and the grains of rice are soft. The aromatic smell of Riz Couché is a giveaway and will waft around your kitchen; enticing your senses. The most delicious part is the rice that sticks to the bottom of the pot. Don't discard it! Wash your hands and dive right in!

PROCEDURE

- Combine rice and stew in a pot.
- Mix them well and warm them up at low heat for 15 to 20 minutes.
- Serve and eat hot.

CAFÉ, PAIN-BEURRE

(Serves 1)

YOU WILL NEED

- Powdered Milk (Nestlé Nido preferred)
- Beurre Président, omelet or chocolate butter spread
- 1 cup of hot water
- 1-2 teaspoons of sugar or 1 or 2 *carreaux* de sucre (two sugar cubes)
- 1 baguette of French bread or toast bread

PROCEDURE

- Put 1 pack of tea or 1 – 2 teaspoons of cocoa or 1 teaspoon of coffee in the mug. Add the sugar.
- Add 1 tablespoon of powdered milk and fill with hot water. Mix the drink.
- Spread the butter of choice on the bread.
- Savor with the café. Enjoy!

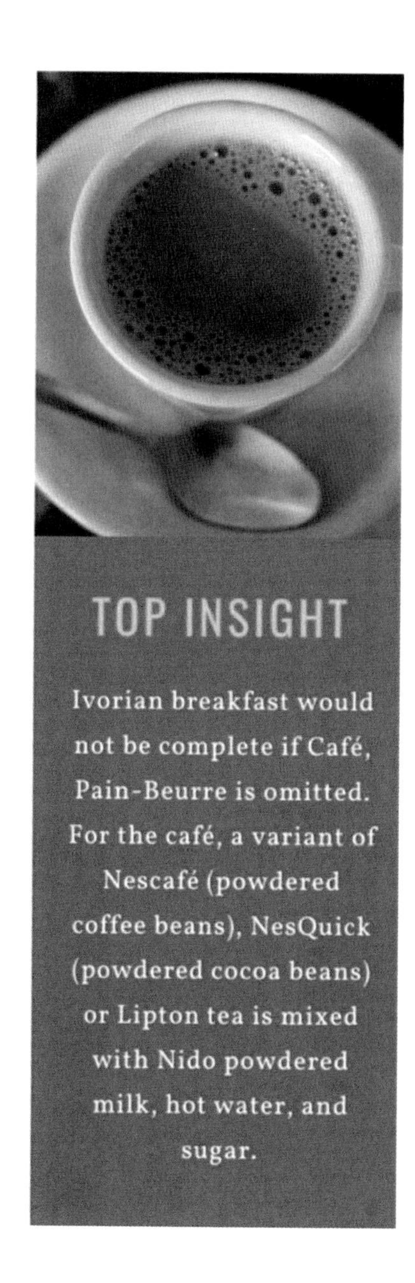

PAIN AVEC DES CONDIMENTS

Sandwiches

(Serves 1-4)

YOU WILL NEED

- 1 baguette of bread or 1 croissant
- Sides such as guacamole, tomato sauces with different types of meat and fish, boiled eggs, etc.

TOP INSIGHT

Pain avec des Condiments is an all-time favorite for students of all grades. Caterers of these goodies lign up daily in front and in school establishments to sell their plethora of sides with breads. There are a hit!

PROCEDURE

- Spread the condiments in the breads and enjoy.

COCO BACCA

Bouillie de Mil ou Maïs Fermenté Sans Grains

(Serves 4-6)

YOU WILL NEED

- 2 cups of the flour desired
- 1 pureed ginger root
- 1 – 2 teaspoons of cayenne pepper
- 1 – 2 teaspoons of black pepper
- Powdered or condensed milk (optional)
- 1 cup of sugar
- 6 cups of water
- 1 glass of water

PROCEDURE

- Mix all the ingredients except the glass of water and milk and let it sit for thirty-six hours to ferment.
- After thirty-six hours, the flour paste will settle at the bottom of your container. Remove the water with tact and bring it to boil.
- Add a glass of water to the paste of water and add it quickly to the boiling water.
- Cook it for another 5 to 10 minutes, serve and eat!
- You can also season your porridge to liking with yoghurt, powdered or condensed milk.

TOP INSIGHT

Coco Bacca is a variant of Kabba Bacca or Gnomi Bacca. However, this porridge is without grains. It's very spicy and sold on the streets of Ivory Coast. Coco Bacca is always served hot. Our favorite type is the purple (blue) corn Coco Bacca. Unfortunately, this flour is hard to come by. Nonetheless, check out the one below. You can eat it with gnomi or millet beignets. Sorghum's powder can also be made into Coco-Bacca.

QUAKER OR FLOCONS D'AVOINE

Oatmeal

(Serves 2-4)

YOU WILL NEED

- 1 cup of your preferred oats
- 1 cup of water for instant oats. Add more water for steel-cuts and rolled oats
- Sugar to taste
- Milk, yoghurt, noix de cannelle (cinnamon), dried raisins are optional

PROCEDURE

- Bring water to boil and add oats.
- Stir occasionally.
- Cook until tender.
- Remove from heat and serve.
- Season to liking and eat.

TOP INSIGHT

Quaker oats are very enjoyed by Ivorians who can afford to buy this cereal. Compared to the prevalence of instant oats in the United States, Ivorians like to eat rolled oats. Whether you prefer steel-cut, rolled oats or instant oats, it's fine as long as you're able to make breakfast out of it.

BEVERAGES

"Bissap always reminds me of primary school in Yamousskro by The Lakes of Caimans."— A. Fofana

BISSAP

Roselle Juice or Hibiscus Flower Juice

(Serves 1-4)

YOU WILL NEED

- 1 cup of dry *bissap* leaves
- 1 lemon
- 1 liter of hot water
- 1 - 2 tablespoons of dried mint or 1 bunch of fresh mint leaves
- 1 cup of sugar
- 1 packet of vanilla sugar
- 1 cup of pineapple juice (optional)

PROCEDURE

- In a large container, add *bissap*, hot water and the mint.
- Let the mixture sit for a couple hours.
- Use a sieve to separate the leaves from the juice.
- Add sugars, lemon and pineapple. Season to taste with more things if needed.
- Serve cold. And voilà!

TOP INSIGHT

Bissap or Oseille is also known as Jamaican flower juice. It's a very refreshing drink packed with Vitamin C. In other places of West Africa such as Nigeria and Senegal, it's call Zobo or Sobolo. It tastes a bit like tart cherry juice. Oseille's leaves are also used for a stew.

GNANMANKOUDJI

Ginger Juice

(Serves 1-2)

YOU WILL NEED

- 1 large root of fresh ginger
- 1 lemon
- 1 - 2 tablespoons of dried mint or 1 bunch of fresh mint leaves
- 1 cup of sugar
- 1 packet of vanillin sugar
- 1 cup of pineapple or orange juice (optional)
- 1 liter of water

PROCEDURE

- In a food processor, purée the ginger root.
- In a large container, add the ginger, water and the mint.
- Let the mixture sit for 30 minutes to an hour.
- Use a sieve to collect only the juice.
- Add sugars, lemon and pineapple. Season to taste with more things if needed.
- Serve cold.
- Enjoy!

TOP INSIGHT

Gnanmankoudji is a sweet spicy drink consumed cold in Ivory Coast. It helps with diseases such as the common cold and boosts the immune system.

TOMI-DJI

Tamarind Juice

(Serves 1-2)

YOU WILL NEED

- 3 - 5 long pods of Tomi (Tamarind)
- 1 lemon
- A pinch of salt
- 1 cup of sugar
- 1 packet of vanilla sugar
- 1.5 liters of water

TOP INSIGHT

Tomi-dji is another popular drink in the streets and households of Ivory Coast. If you had peach juice before, you will notice the similarity. It's tangy, sweet and salty at the same time. Dji means water in Mandingue (Mandé.) In this case, it means juice.

PROCEDURE

- Boil the Tomi with the water for 5 to 10 mins and let it cool down.
- In a large container, pour the mixture.
- With your right fingers, mash the pods to release the pulp. Every seed should be naked.
- Use a sieve to collect the juice.
- Add sugars, salt, and lemon.
- Season to taste with more things if needed.

YAHOURT

Yoghurt

(Serves 6-12)

YOU WILL NEED

- ¾ to 1 gallon of milk
- One 3.8 to 1 liter Pyrex vase with a lid
- A tablecloth or long rectangular wrap
- 3 tablespoons of plain yoghurt
- A large pan to boil the milk. Tip*: A thin or light pan boils faster than a thicker one.
- Sugar and vanilla sugar to taste

PROCEDURE

- Boil the milk on medium heat for 15 to 30 minutes.
- Stir every 5 to 10 minutes so that the milk doesn't stick to the pan and burn.
- Remove milk from heat when starting to foam and rise or when very hot.
- Pour it in the deep Pyrex vase and let it cool down (lukewarm) from about 20 to 30 minutes. When still lukewarm, add in the yoghurt (the starter) and stir well.
- Close lid and wrap the vase in the tablecloth.
- Store in a warm place or inside the oven. Make sure you look into your oven before warming up going forward if that's the place you chose to store your yoghurt. Four hours is the minimum time to make yoghurt. We usually put ours around 8 or 9 p.m. and we don't get it out until the next morning after 6 a.m. Sweeten and dilute to taste.

TOP INSIGHT

Yoghurt is a favorite thing to sell in cellophane bags for small business owners. It generates revenue because consumers love its tarp, creamy and refreshing nature. It can be sold in popsicle formats (Yaourt Grotto) as well. If making Yaourt Grotto, use the wooden stick once the ice pop is frozen, to stir the popsicle in the mold a couple times. Then, use a table knife to insert between the Yaourt and the interior of the mold. It makes it easy to remove. Now, pull it out fast and eat the popsicle.

DÊGUÊ

Sweetened Couscous of Millet in Yoghurt

(Serves 2-3)

YOU WILL NEED

- 1 cup of dry steamed millet couscous grains
- 1 glass of water
- A teaspoon of butter
- 4 cups of Greek yoghurt or thick plain yoghurt
- 2 cups of sweetened condensed milk or sugar
- 1 to 2 cups of dried raisins (optional)
- A pinch of nutmeg (optional)

PROCEDURE

- Add a glass of water to the millet grains and let them boil until the grains are soft.
- Then add a little butter and let them sit to cool down.
- Mix the yoghurt and the condensed milk until the mixture is uniform.
- Add the millet grains to the sweetened yoghurt and mix.
- Taste and add more sugar if necessary.
- Finally, add the dried raisins and a pinch of nutmeg if desired.
- Refrigerate and serve cold.
- Enjoy!

TOP INSIGHT

Dègué (Dêguê) is another favorite dessert and beverage in West Africa. While Gnomi is mostly seasonal, Dègué is not. It's sold everywhere in the streets of Ivory Coast but only those who have strong digestive systems buy it outside. It's milk-based and that alone makes it a dangerous substance if not stored properly. Therefore, many people opt out of buying it in the streets. On the other hand, it's a very common dish gifted during Ramadan. During this time, everyone knows the gifter made it herself because that is what most women do during Ramadan; they usually outdo themselves in the kitchen.

THÉ DE CITRONELLE

Lemon Grass Tea

(Serves 2-3)

YOU WILL NEED

- 1 small bunch of thé de citronelle
- 1 liter of water
- ½ of a cup of sugar
- Honey (optional)

PROCEDURE

- In a teapot or kettle, boil the water and the washed leaves for 10 - 20 minutes
- Add sugar or honey to taste.
- Serve and drink in a mug.

TOP INSIGHT

Thé de Citronelle is a multi-purpose drink in Ivory Coast. It's consumed to relax and to treat some diseases. If you can't find the leaves, you can substitute this tea with a packet of Boh Lemon Myrtle Tea and 1 cup of hot water. It has lemon grass in its constitution.

CHOUGBAN

Kinkéliba

(Serves 2-3)

YOU WILL NEED

- 1/4 of a cup of dried *chougban* leaves
- 1 liter of water
- ½ of a cup of sugar or to taste.
- Honey (optional)

PROCEDURE

- In a teapot or kettle, boil the water and the washed leaves for 10 - 20 minutes
- Add sugar or honey to taste.
- Serve and drink in a mug.

TOP INSIGHT

Kinkéliba is another multi-purpose tea that helps with digestion or other ailments. It is said to promote a long and healthy life. It has more healing properties than green tea, and it's well known in West Africa.

TAPIOCA

Granulated Cassava Grains

(Serves 2-3)

YOU WILL NEED

- 1 cup of white tapioca pearls
- 3 - 4 cups of water
- 1 -2 cups of sugar
- 1 cup of liquid milk (optional)
- Sucre vanillé-vanillin sugar (optional)
- Powdered or condensed milk (optional)
- Plain yoghurt (optional)

PROCEDURE

- Bring water to boil.
- Add pearls and stir.
- Cook for another 5 - 10 mins. Pearls should be really soft and look like a pudding. Add liquid milk, and sugars. Let it simmer for another 5 - 10 mins.
- When time elapses, serve and eat. It can be served hot or cold.
- You can also season your tapioca to your liking with yoghurt, powdered or condensed milk.

TOP INSIGHT

Tapioca is a starchy beverage made from cassava roots. The pearls are boiled and consumed with milk and sugar. It's an easy and straightforward recipe if we say so ourselves.

GARI

Pre-Cooked Cassava Semolina

(Serves 1-2)

YOU WILL NEED

- 1 cup of yellow gari
- 1 - 2 cups of water
- 1 - 2 tablespoons of sugar
- 1 cup of liquid milk (optional)
- Powdered or condensed milk (optional)
- Plain yoghurt (optional)

PROCEDURE

- Mix water to Gari.
- Add sugar, milk and stir.
- You can also season your instant Gari to your liking with yoghurt, powdered or condensed milk.

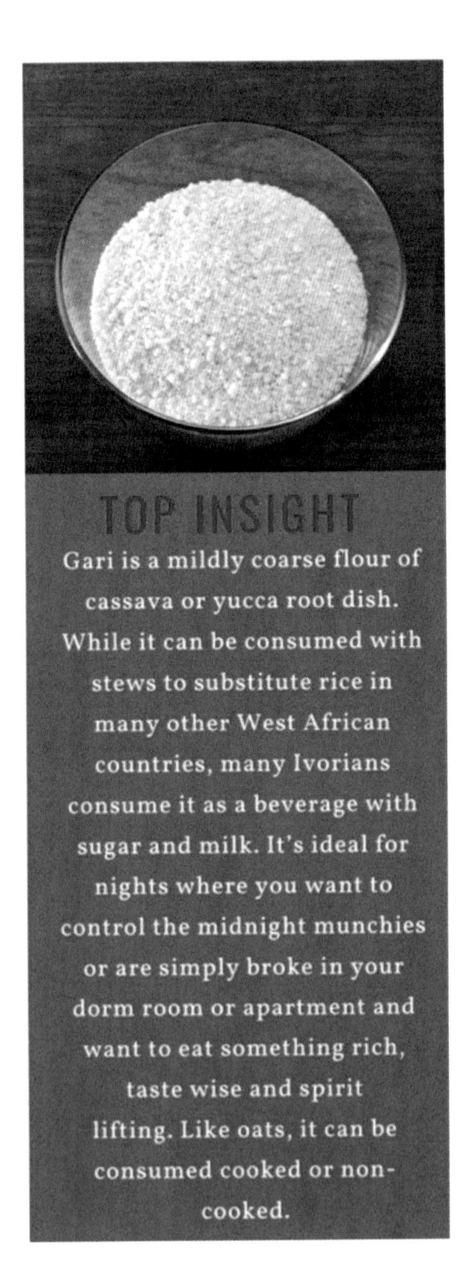

SIROPS

Sirups

(Serves 1)

YOU WILL NEED

- 1 tablespoon of any sirup listed in the top insight section below
- ½ of a cup of milk (optional)
- ¼ of cup of water
- Ice cubes to taste
- Fresh mint leaves for garnish

TOP INSIGHT

Though not authentic Ivorian drinks, sirups of mint, grenadine and strawberry are very popular drinks in Ivory Coast's events and households. If you want to feel posh in Ivory Coast, you will serve these drinks to your guests. You can also turn ginger or roselle juices into sirups too. You just need to boil them to turn them into a thick liquid. Store in a glass bottle.

PROCEDURE

- Mix all the ingredients.
- Taste and add more of the ingredients to your liking.
- Garnish and serve cold.

FOFKY'S COFFEE AND TEA DRINKS

(Serves 1-2)

TOP INSIGHT

Fofky's Mixes are easy chocolate, coffees and teas that you can purchase and follow instructions to make hot and cool drinks. They include lattes, frappuccinos, machiattos, mochas, and teas—bobas and plant based. Ivory Coast is one of the world top producers of cocoa and coffee. So check this Ivorian heritage out at www.fofkys.com.

Tip*: You can extract cocoa beans' juice by dumping the contents of a pod or pods in a sieve. Place a container below the sieve to collect the juice.

On the other hand, you can also boil coffee fruit's cherries without the seeds to consume as a tea; Cascara. Enjoy!

YOU WILL NEED

- 1 Fofky's Mix sachet

PROCEDURE

- Blend Fofky's Mix with five cubes of ice or six oz. of hot water
- Serve, garnish, and drink.

GRILLADES
OR
APPETIZERS & STARTERS

"Garba always reminded me of my early university days with my classmates. Every Friday, we put money together and met for lunch to savor Garba Choco with gusto."
— Nabintou bint Youssef

Meats in Ivory Coast are always boiled, smoked, in the following formats in the *grillades* sections and etc. and etc...

Poisson (Fish)
- Frit (Fried)
- Braisé (Braised)

Viande de bœuf (Beef)
- Frit
- Braisé

Poulet (Chicken)
- Frit
- Braisé

Dindon (Turkey)
- Frit
- Braisé

Viande de moutton (Lamb)
- Frit
- Braisé

Rognons (Kidneys)
- Frit
- Braisé

Foie (liver) de poulet, bœuf ou moutton
- Frit
- Braisé

Pintade (Quail)
- Frit
- Braisé

There are other types of meat consumed not listed above; they fall into the bush meat category. We won't cover them in this cookbook.

Marinated Chicken

Gas Oven Braised Chicken

ALLOCO POISSON FRIT

Fried Plantain Banana with Fried Fish

Serves (1-2)

YOU WILL NEED

- 3 ripe bananas
- 1 liter of oil to fry
- 1 fish carp
- Salt to taste
- Black pepper or lemon pepper to taste
- Cayenne pepper to taste

PROCEDURE

- Peel the bananas and cut them in any shape you want.
- Season them with a pinch of salt and get ready to fry them.
- Clean the fish and season it with the peppers.
- When the oil is hot, fry the bananas and the fish separetely.
- Remove when cooked and golden.

TOP INSIGHT

Alloco Poisson Frit is perhaps the most known Ivorian dish. The fish can be braised too. This dish is served with a hot pepper and tomato sauce called Piment. Piment, in its right use of the word, means pepper. Alloco can also be served with other tubes such as Frites de Pomme de Terre (French Fries) and a wide range of proteins such as boiled eggs and other fried and braised meats. Tip*: A deep fryer is a wonderful investment with Ivorian Cuisine. In Latin America countries, they eat Alloco with ice cream. It's a dessert for them and a great discovery made at an *iftar* dinner with another inter-racial couple from the United States.

IGNAME FRIT

Fried Yam

Serves (1-2)

YOU WILL NEED

- 1 medium yam
- 1 liter of oil to fry
- Salt to taste

PROCEDURE

- Peel the yam and cut it in any shape you want.
- Season the pieces with a pinch of salt and get ready to fry them.
- When the oil is hot, fry the yams.
- Remove when cooked and golden.
- Eat with any side.

TOP INSIGHT

Igname Frit is a great afternoon or evening nibble. Serve with any meat or fish dishes. You can also fry sweet yams; the white and orange ones. You can braise these tubers too. Tip*: Make sure the fresh peel of a white yam doesn't touch the outer skin of your hands! This peel is itchy!!!

IGNAME BOUILLIE

Boiled Yam

Serves (1-2)

YOU WILL NEED

- 1 medium yam
- Enough water to cover the yams
- Salt
- 1 habanero pepper for aroma

PROCEDURE

- Peel the yam and cut it in any shape you want.
- Add some salt, the fresh pepper and get ready to boil them.
- Remove when cooked and soft.
- Use a fork to check their readiness.

TOP INSIGHT

Igname Bouillie can be served with a plethora of things such as de la Pâte de Poisson — seasoned fish sauce, seasoned lamb, beef and etc. Even sardines work. It's an easy dish to make that will keep you full for a while. Yams are something you can also eat with simply oil and salt. They are purely satisfying.

BANANE BOUILLIE

Boiled Plantain Banana

Serves (1)

YOU WILL NEED

- 1 medium ripe banana
- Enough water to cover the plantains
- Salt

PROCEDURE

- Peel the plantain and cut it in any shape you want.
- Add some salt and get ready to boil them.
- Remove when cooked and soft.
- Use a fork to check their readiness.

TOP INSIGHT

Banane Bouillie is another dish can be served with a plethora of things such as palm nut oil, de la Pâte de Poisson— seasoned fish sauce, seasoned lamb, beef, etc. Even sardines work. It's an easy dish to make that will keep you full for a while. Other tubers that can be boiled are sweet yams and cassava (yucca roots.)

ATTIEKÉ

Cassava Couscous

Serves (3)

TOP INSIGHT

Attiéké is made from fresh cassava paste. The paste is fermented and steamed to arrive to the final product. Another close derivative is Attoukou (Atoupkou or Atchoukou). They both look similar only that Attoukou is a pancake of Attiéké. The grains of Attoukou are stickier than its cousin Attiéké and have been steamed a little further in a regular pancake shape. Attoukou tastes great with stews, especially Sauce Aubergine. Check out some fresh Attiéké in the background straight from the motherland. In the streets of Ivory Coast, it's sold in large banana leaves. The leaves can also serve as plates because there are non-porous.
Tip*: always have a glass of water next to you when eating Attiéké. It has the tendency of getting stuck in throats. Tread carefully with this delicious dish!

GARBA AU POISSON THON

Cassava Couscous with Tuna Fish

Serves (1)

YOU WILL NEED

- 1 frozen or fresh bag of *attiéké*. 1 pack of dry *attiéké* works too.
- 1 slice of fresh tuna fish
- Salt to taste
- 1 green habanero pepper
- ½ an onion
- 1 Cube Maggi Étoile
- 1 - 2 tablespoons of oil

PROCEDURE

- Warm the *attiéké au bain-marie.*
- Use a fork to check the readiness.
- Add some salt, oil, diced peppers, and onions.

TOP INSIGHT

Garba is *attiéké* with fried tuna fish. It's served with diced or sliced habanero peppers. You can buy the tuber couscous at any African store.

Garba is usually sold in the streets of Ivory Coast with only habanero peppers, diced onions, fried tuna fish, Cube Maggi Étoile and some oil as seasoning. You can add other vegetables if needed but you don't have to. Stir fry a can of tuna in case you don't have fresh tuna fish. It's tuna! Check out the tuna fish salad and *attiéké* to the left of the page. The mix of the two plates is called Salade Bassamoise—Salad from Bassam in some parts of Ivory Coast. Grand-Bassam is a coastal resort town stretching along the Atlantic Ocean. It's located at the east of Abidjan; the economical capital of Ivory Coast. During colonial times, Grand-Bassam was an Ivorian capital for three years; from 1893-1896.

ATTIEKÉ POISSON FRIT

Cassava Couscous with Fried Fish

Serves (1)

YOU WILL NEED

- 1 frozen or fresh bag of *attiéké*. 1 pack of dry *attiéké* works too.
- 1 whole fish (Carp preferred)
- Salt to taste
- 1 ripe tomato
- ½ an onion
- 1 Cube Maggi Étoile
- 1 - 2 tablespoons of oil
- ½ a cucumber
- 1 - 3 teaspoons of vinegar

TOP INSIGHT

Attiéké Poisson Frit looks like Garba. The difference is the type of fish used. Here, the fish is any fish except tuna fish.You can also use braised fish to eat this dish. And any *attiéké* recipe is not complete if Cube Maggi Étoile is not added to it. It gives it a special taste recognizable anywhere. It's perhaps one of the only two occasions we use a bouillon in **Fofky's Kitchen**. We would like to promote a healthier lifestyle composed of less salt and artificial ingredients.
On other hand, it's important to note that *attiéké* is often mistaken for fine bulgur—cracked wheat.
Finally, *attiéké* has a delicious aftertaste that is a bit sour.

PROCEDURE

- Warm the *attiéké au bain-marie.*
- Use a fork to check the readiness.
- In another bowl, add some salt, oil, vinegar, diced tomatoes, cucumbers, peppers and onions.
- Stir and serve with the *attiéké* and the fried fish of your liking.

CUIS DE DINDON

Turkey Tails

Serves (4)

YOU WILL NEED

- 1 bag of fresh or frozen Turkey tails
- 1 - 3 cloves of garlic
- 1 teaspoon of salt
- 1 teaspoon of black pepper
- 1 -2 tablespoons of vinegar or 1 - 2 tablespoons of mustard
- 1 bunch of parsley
- ½ an onion
- 1 teaspoon of cayenne or ground red pepper
- 1 green onion
- Rosemary (optional)

PROCEDURE

- In a food processor, blend the garlic, parsley, and the onions.
- Transfer the mixture in a large container.
- Add the washed meat, salt, spices, vinegar and mustard. Mix well and let it sit for at least an hour.
- When time elapses, bake, fry, roast or braise to your liking. You can eat the meat with anything such as French bread, *attiéké*, yams, *alloco*, etc.

TOP INSIGHT

Cuis de Dindon or Turkey tails are extremely hard to find but not impossible. Small towns often have it in their groceries but don't bet on that. If you happen to find them around the holiday season because it's a bit seasonal, you're in luck. There are easy to make and can be braised, fried, roasted or boiled.

CHOUKOUYA OR BROCHETTES

Skewers

Serves (4)

YOU WILL NEED

- 1 lb of any diced meat
- 1 - 3 cloves of garlic
- 1 teaspoon of salt
- 1 teaspoon of black pepper
- 1 bag of wooden skewers
- 1 - 2 tablespoons of mustard
- 1 small bunch of fresh parsley
- ½ an onion
- 1 teaspoon of cayenne or ground red pepper
- 1 small bunch of fresh green onion
- 1/4 of a cup of Kankankan spice (Mix equal portions of chili, cinnamon, kola nut, ginger and pepper powders.)

PROCEDURE

- In a food processor, blend the garlic, parsley, green onion, and regular onion.
- Transfer the mixture in a large container.
- Add the washed meat, salt, spices and mustard. Mix well and let the marinade sit for at least an hour.
- When time elapses, thread the meat onto the skewers and grill or bake them for 30 to 60 minutes. Garnish with Kankankan spice.

TOP INSIGHT

Choukouya is the thing to eat in the afternoon around 4 p.m. in Ivory Coast. These vendors' stalls are crowded around that time of the day. They are a hit!

To make yourself, wooden skewers need to be soaked in water for at least 20 minutes before grilling. They are best enjoyed inside baguettes of breads. Choukouya can also be served with *attiéké*, yams, *alloco*, etc.

ESCARGOTS

Snails

Serves (5-6)

YOU WILL NEED

- 10 - 12 edible escargots
- 1 - 3 cloves of garlic
- 1 teaspoon of salt
- 1 teaspoon of black pepper
- 1 bag of wooden skewers
- 1 - 2 tablespoons of mustard
- 1 small bunch of fresh parsley
- ½ an onion
- 1 teaspoon of cayenne pepper
- 1 small bunch of fresh green onion
- Rosemary (optional)

TOP INSIGHT

Eating Escargots is a thing that sprouts a lot of controversial discussions in Ivory Coast especially if you're Muslim. Some consider it dirty because it has a lot of saliva and others believe it's edible. Many Muslims who want to eat it go to great length to make it edible. They pour a lot of salt on it and let it sit. This sanitizes it in the first step of the cleaning process. Then, they wash it well and clean it. Next, they lay it on top of the cover of a boiling pot. The content of the pot is not important; they just need the the heat of the pot to dry the saliva from the meat of escargot. Every few seconds, you will hear a frying sound that comes from the saliva being removed and the escargot becoming dehydrated. The meat is ready to be processed further in any dish when no more saliva emanates from the dehydrated escargot. Now, the escargots can be used in a stew, fried, braised, etc. and made into any dish of the consumer liking. Escargots on skewers or in palm nut stew are a thing to try for sure. It's up to you to make your decision to eat them.

PROCEDURE

- In a food processor, blend the garlic, parsley, and green onion, and onion.
- Transfer the mixture in a large container.
- Add the washed meat, salt, spices and mustard. Mix well and let it sit for at least an hour.
- When time elapses, thread the meet onto the skewers and grill or bake them for 30 to 60 minutes. You can also prepare them with a spicy sauce like in the picture to the right.

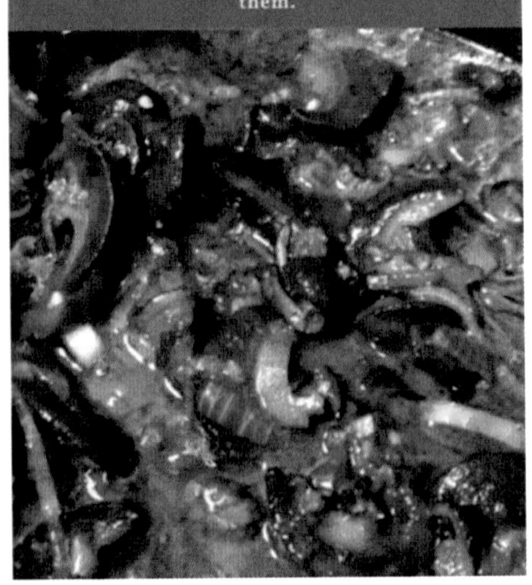

ROGNONS

Spicy Kidneys

Serves (4-6)

YOU WILL NEED

- 1 pound of beef kidneys
- 1 - 3 diced cloves of garlic
- 1 teaspoon of salt
- 1 teaspoon of black pepper
- 1 - 3 diced habanero peppers
- 1- 2 tablespoons of mustard
- 1 small bunch of fresh parsley
- 1 diced onion
- 2 diced tomatoes
- 1 teaspoon of cayenne pepper or ground red pepper
- 1 small bunch of fresh green onion diced
- Rosemary (optional)
- 1 - 3 tablespoons of olive oil
- 1 - 3 glasses of water

PROCEDURE

- Rinse the kidneys and trim any fat on it. Then, cut the meat in medium pieces.
- When done, boil the pieces of kidneys until soft and cooked.
- Next, sautéed the kidneys with salt, diced garlic, long slices of onions, and diced tomatoes until golden.
- Add the rest of the ingredients and let it cook for 15 - 20 minutes at low to medium heat.
- Remove from heat and serve.

TOP INSIGHT

Much like Choukouya, Rognons are very popular in the streets of Ivory Coast. It's mainly served with the famous *attiéké*. This dish is supposed to be spicy. Livers and gizzards can be made this way too but with less hot peppers.

SNACKS

"Street Food was often forbidden by our parents. However, there were times our parents allowed us to eat out. Abga Klaklo or Plantain Klaklo were often at the top of the list when we had the green light from them."— H. bint Youssef

BLISSI TEBIL OR
BANANE BRAISÉE AVEC ARACHIDE GRILLÉ
Roasted Plantain Bananas with Toasted Nuts
(Serves 1)

TOP INSIGHT

Blissi Tebil is simply the name of roasted bananas accompanied with roasted peanuts. It's sold almost everywhere in the streets of Ivory Coast. It's always hot and ready to eat. You can never go wrong with this nibble. The name comes from a former celebrity by the name of Blissi Tebil. He told the media that he was on a food strike because the social conditions of artists back then sucked. Later the same day, snoopy people saw him break his fast with this snack. For that reason, the dish has been renamed with his name. Some gas ovens have a broiler drawer that many people use as storage. If you have such an oven, it's the best part of the oven to use to braise your plantains and even meats in this cookbook!

YOU WILL NEED

- 1 - 3 ripe plantain bananas
- 1 cup of roasted salted Spanish peanuts. They are also called redskin Spanish peanuts in case you have a hard time finding them.

PROCEDURE

- Peel the plantains and braise them directly on your oven rack.
- Flip them every 5 to 10 minutes. Serve after 20 to 60 minutes depending on your oven.
- Enjoy with the nuts. You can also warm the nuts by baking them for a few minutes.

KLAKLO

Plantain Fritters

(Serves 1)

TOP INSIGHT

Klaklo is consumed with Piment; a hot and seasoned tomato, onion and pepper sauce.

Another type of klaklo or gnomi that is great for snack is Sosso Mommi—White Bean Fritters. In this recipe, the powder of the beans is used. Even though, we grew up eating it, it's a dish more popular in countries such as Burkina Faso.

YOU WILL NEED

For the Klaklo

- 1-3 of really ripe plantain bananas
- ½ an onion & 1 liter or frying oil
- Salt & Pepper to taste
- 1 tomato & 1 clove of garlic

For the Piment

- 1 onion
- 2 tomatoes
- 1 clove of garlic
- Salt, Pepper, Cube Maggi Étoile to taste
- 3 tablespoons of olive oil

PROCEDURE

- Blend all the ingredients of Klaklo. You should get a uniform paste like depicted in the picture on the side in the small transparent glass bowl.
- With a spoon or your right hand, drop dollops of the paste into the heated deep fryer. Keep doing this until your whole mixture is finished. Cook on medium heat until the plantain fritters turn browny red and remove to set aside.
- Blend all the ingredients of the Piment. Heat the oil and pour the mixture in it. Decrease the heat. Rapidly stir and remove within 5 - 10 minutes. Serve and enjoy your Klaklo au Piment!

EXTRAS

Other Snacks

(Serves 1 -2)

TOP INSIGHT

Pokis are Ivorian Kool Aid bursts and Fun Pops. They come in many shapes such as fish and corn cob shapes contrarily to Koo Aid Bursts which come in one uniform plastic package.

Yaourt Grotto is sweetened and diluted yoghurt. The container in which it is frozen is made out of metal. It's actually a small baking tin. A wooden stick is inserted in it to facilitate the removal and selling to the client. You can use a muffin pan and wooden popsicle sticks to make this snack. Just sweeten your plain yoghurt, add a bit of water, pour it in the muffin mold, add your popsicle stick, freeze for an hour or two and voilà! Tip*: There is a recipe in this book to make your own yoghurt. Check it out.

Gâteaux au Four are really sweet small muffins. The tins for the previous snack can be used here. They have somewhat the same shape.

Bonbon Ta Main Cole is a hard candy shaped in the form of a cone. It has a caramelly color and it's very sticky. It's made of candied sugar and other obscure ingredients. The last part is just to make you laugh. But it's true. On the other hand, it tastes a bit like Manisu Mesir Macunu; a Turkish toffi made of forty-one spices.

Baobab Powder is sold in paper cones to consume as a snack. It's tightly closed and it has usually been filtered to remove the fibers in its powder. Some granulated sugar is normally added to it to sweeten it. The folded paper cone container acts like a pucker powder fun tube.

Boiled eggs and salted ground red pepper are also a treat!

We mention some of these just to give you cultural insights about Ivorian Cuisine. And truly, there are way too many snacks in the streets of Ivory Coast and not enough pages to include them in this book.

Baobab Powder

Yaourt Grotto

ARACHIDE BOUILLIE

Boiled Peanuts

(Serves 1)

TOP INSIGHT

This is the snack extraordinaire enjoyed during heated discussions and chats! You will notice the same trend with American Baseball fans at the game.

YOU WILL NEED

- 2 cups of raw peanuts with the shell
- 3 cups of water
- Salt to taste (optional)

PROCEDURE

- Wash the fresh peanuts well to remove any dirt.
- Put all the ingredients in a medium size pot and bring the *mélange* to boil.
- Check the readiness of your peanuts by opening a shell and eating the peanuts. It shouldn't take more 20 or 30 minutes to cook depending on the freshness of your batch of peanuts.

CACAHUÈTES

Caramelized Candied Peanuts

(Serves 1-2)

TOP INSIGHT

Cacahuètes is a delicious snack to combat sugar cravings. There are very affordable and easy to make. They are essentially the same as *garrapiñada.*

YOU WILL NEED

- 2 cups of raw peanuts with the skin
- 1 cup of sugar
- ½ a cup of water

PROCEDURE

- Put all the ingredients in a medium size pot and bring the *mélange* to boil at low heat.
- As the water evaporates, the sugar will crystallize.
- Stir fast and continuously until the peanuts are coated.
- Cool down, serve or store in a glass container.

AGBA KLAKLO OR BOULE BOULE DE MANIOC AU COCO

Cassava Fritters

(Serves 1-2)

TOP INSIGHT

Agba Klaklo is a rich snack reminiscent a little bit of tater tots. The coconut slices embellish the taste further. Try it in your kitchen, it doesn't take long to make.

YOU WILL NEED

- 1 fresh cassava root (yucca root)
- 1 - 2 cups of diced and dried coconut flesh
- 1 liter of frying oil
- ½ a teaspoon of salt
- 3 - 5 tablespoons of olive oil
- 1 tablespoon of yeast (optional.) If using, add it with the salt.

PROCEDURE

- Peel the root, gut it, wash, and cut it in several pieces.
- Grate it or use a food processor to turn it into a paste. When done, place the paste into a rag.
- Put the rag into a sieve and let the root's juice drip (Optional because there won't be much juice in it.)
- When the paste is not too wet but just right, transfer it into a larger container.
- Add the salt and the olive oil.
- Then, roll the mixture into small balls. Continue until you finish the whole paste.
- Now, fry and remove when cooked and golden.

CHIPS DE BANANE

Plantain Banana Chips

(Serves 3-6)

TOP INSIGHT

Chips de Banane make great afternoon snacks. They taste better with non-ripe plantain bananas. However, these chips can be made with ripe plantains too. The ripe are sweet of course.

YOU WILL NEED

- 1 - 3 green plantain bananas
- Salt to taste
- 1 liter of frying oil

PROCEDURE

- Peel the plantains and slice them thinly.
- Salt them and heat the oil.
- Fry them and remove when golden and crisp.

CROQUETTES

Dry Cakes

(Serves 3-6)

TOP INSIGHT

Also known as Chin-Chin or Gateaux Sec, Croquettes are a hit anywhere in Ivory Coast for snacks. From school establishments to large African parties, this snack is everywhere to entertain the guests.

YOU WILL NEED

- 1 - 2 cups of flour
- 1 egg
- 1 liter of frying oil
- ½ a cup of butter
- 1 - 2 tablespoons of powdered milk
- 1 - 2 tablespoons of nutmeg

PROCEDURE

- Mix flour, sugar and nutmeg in a large container.
- Add in the melted butter.
- Add the egg and milk. Mix the mixture well. The dough shouldn't be sticky. Add more flour if it's sticky.
- Then, divide the dough in equal portions and roll them into long ropes.
- Cut them into small squares and fry.
- Remove when brown and crisp.

CARAMEL

Peanut Brittle

(Serves 1-2)

TOP INSIGHT

Caramel is a sweet snack that was always considered contraband in our school classrooms because it was a distracting agent during lectures. It was also sold by other classmates who were not approved vendors. While these classmates made some pocket change on Caramel, it was often confiscated. Other snacks also faced the same challenge. And much like the other snacks, it's very popular all over Ivory Coast. This nougat is very easy to make but it requires a high level of skill and speed.

YOU WILL NEED

- 1 .5 cups of fried nuts
- 1 cup of sugar
- 1 cup of oil to roll the brittle

PROCEDURE

- In a food processor, chop the nuts.
- Then, at low heat, melt the sugar and slowly add the chopped nuts when the sugar turns to a caramel color.
- Stir fast.
- When the mixture is uniform, pour it on an oily surface and roll it flat with a rolling pin. Be quick because it will harden fast.
- With a sharp knife, cut it into trapeze or any shape you like.
- Serve or store in a glass jar.

TOFFI

Hard Candy

(Serves 20)

TOP INSIGHT

Toffi is another popular snack and a treasured bonbon. There are many shapes of Toffi in the streets of Ivory Coast and you can design yours to your liking. Many types of Toffi in the streets are packaged like sausage links to facilitate the selling. This recipe is designed for the marble looking Toffi and you're welcome to tweak it. Toffi is also made out of coconut milk. This type of Toffi is saltier.

YOU WILL NEED

- 1 can of sweetened condensed milk
- 1 tablespoon of olive oil for the toffi mixture (optional)
- 1 tablespoon of olive oil to roll the toffi
- 1 teaspoon of vanillin sugar
- 1 - 2 tablespoons of water

PROCEDURE

- At low to medium heat, put 1 tablespoon of oil in a pan and add in the milk.
- Constantly stir with a spatula.
- When the mixture is brown, add in the water and continue stirring until the milk is a uniform brown ball.
- Transfer it on an oily surface, cut and roll small pieces from the batch with oily hands until done. Be quick because it will harden fast.
- Serve or store in a glass jar.

COCO GRILLÉ

Grilled Grated Coconut

(Serves 1-2)

TOP INSIGHT

Coco Grillé is sweet and sold in cellophane bags or glass jars. It's a snack enjoyed with a cool and refreshing drink such as Bissap, Gnanmankoudji, Tomi-dji, etc. Guess what! You can now make it yourself if you didn't know in less than thirty minutes! Coco Grillé can also be made soft and shaped into balls like cake pops.

YOU WILL NEED

- 1 cup of Kosher or organic sweetened shredded coconut

PROCEDURE

- Put ingredients in a skillet on medium heat.
- Stir regularly with a spatula until the shredded coconut threads are brown and crisp.
- You can toast them in the oven on a flat baking sheet for 10 - 15 mins on 300°F.

MAÏS BRAISÉ

Braised Corn

(Serves 1-2)

TOP INSIGHT

Maïs Braisé is like Blissi Tebil; a great noon to afternoon snack. During the corn season, it's a hit in the streets of Ivory Coast.

YOU WILL NEED

- 1 - 2 corns on the cob

PROCEDURE

- Remove husk and silk.
- Keep some of the husk if you want to use it to serve.
- Braise them directly on your oven rack. Use your broiler drawer if you have a gas oven
- Flip it every 5 to 10 minutes.
- Serve on corn husk after 20 to 30 minutes.

TOP INSIGHT

Bon Maïs is an easy recipe. While you can pop in the microwave, many Ivorians still do it old school; in a pot!

YOU WILL NEED

- 1 cup of dry corn kernels
- A pinch of salt
- 1 - 2 tablespoons of olive oil
- 1 - 2 tablespoons of Nestlé Nido powdered milk for garnish (optional).

PROCEDURE

- Mix all ingredients in a good size pot and cover it.
- Turn the heat on the pot to medium. Within 5 - 10 minutes, the kernels will start to pop. Remove from heat when the pot quietens for a few seconds.
- Be quick so that the popcorn doesn't burn.
- Garnish as you like.

BREADS & CEREALS

"Guédégba always reminds me of sunny and bright elementary school days in a small town."— Papatia Feauxzar aka Fofky

GALETTE SUCRÉE EN FLEUR

Rosette Cookies

(Serves 20-40)

TOP INSIGHT

Rosettes are in the family of pancakes and funnel cakes. There are easy enough to make. You will need to purchase a rosette iron to make this savory. There are essentially the same as Scandinavian rosette cookies. How they got on the streets of Ivory Coast is a mystery to us. If you get tired of frying these cokies, save the batter to make French crêpes. Yum!

YOU WILL NEED

- 1 cup of flour
- 1 tablespoons of sugar
- 1 cup of milk
- 1 large egg or 2 medium eggs
- 1 liter of frying oil
- 1 teaspoon of vanilla
- 1/4 to 1/2 teaspoon of salt
- 1 cup of powdered sugar for garnish.

PROCEDURE

- Combine sugar, eggs and salt in a bowl and mix them until smooth.
- Then, add flour, milk and vanilla and beat more.
- Heat oil and dip cleaned rosette iron in it first for two minutes. Then dip 1/4 inch of oily and warm rosette iron in the batter and immediately dip it back in the hot oil. The dough will fry and detach from the iron.
- Remove when golden and crispy. Do the same for the rest of the batter.
- Garnish with powdered sugar.

GNOMI

Millet Beignets

(Serves 1-4)

TOP INSIGHT

Gnomi (Womi or Mommi) are like African Poffertjes. They are very popular in West Africa especially during Ramadan. It's pretty hard to see these beignets in the streets of Ivory Coast outside of the holy month. You will need a Dutch pancake maker. A thin spatula, a wooden skewer or a fork to flip the cakes will do. A silicon brush is optional. You can also use corn flour for this recipe but the result is less sweet and a bit of an acquired taste.

YOU WILL NEED

- 3.5 - 4 cups of millet flour
- 1 cup of water
- 2.5 - 3 cups of sugar
- 1-2 cups of unsweetened rice pudding or porridge
- 1 ripe banana (optional)
- 1 cup of frying oil or a can of oil spray

PROCEDURE

- Add the water to the millet flour and mix the two ingredients. Then add the rice pudding and the sugar. If the mixture is too thick, add more water.
- Now, add the smashed banana to the mixture, mix well and let it sit for 2 to 3 hours. When the time elapses, heat the pancake pan. Spray the insides of the domed molds with oil or use your silicon brush to brush them with oil.
- Fill the half-domes with the batter and flip them within 2 minutes or so. They should be gray and golden. Each cake should take less than five minutes to cook in total. You will need to be fast flipping to prevent them from burning. Repeat the process until you have used up all the batter. And Voilà!

BAGUETTE DE PAIN

French Bread

(Serves 1-4)

TOP INSIGHT

In Ivory Coast, there is a boulangerie at almost every neighborhood corner that sells fresh, hot, and affordable bread. Some variants of the bread in Ivory Coast consist of adding some cassava, corn or soybean flour to the wheat flour. However, wheat French baguette remains the most eaten format. It's important to note that the other three types are a bit of an acquired taste. In Fofky's Kitchen, we make baguettes regularly. And they disappear pretty fast.

YOU WILL NEED

- 1.5 cups of wheat flour
- 1 tablespoon of sugar
- 1 cup of hot water
- 1 tablespoon of olive oil
- ½ a teaspoon of Kosher salt
- 1 tablespoon of yeast

PROCEDURE

- Mix the yeast to the water, add the tablespoon of sugar and let it rise and foam.
- Then, add salt and oil to flour and mix well.
- Next, add the foamy yeast mixture to the flour and mix-knead for 5 minutes.
- Cover the dough and set it aside for at least an hour.
- Then, divide the dough into equal portions and roll them into baguettes.
- Bake at 300°F for 20 to 30 minutes.
- Eat the bread plain or with anything you fancy. Ivorians often fancy vegetable oil and Baguette de Pain as a great afternoon snack. They line the insides of the bread with the oil and start chomping it. This practice is similar to the Italian and Mediterranean appetizers where bread and olive oil are often served before a dish.

GUÉDÉGBA

Fried Stuffed Dough

(Serves 1-6)

TOP INSIGHT

Guédégba is an asymetrical stuffed fried dough that we enjoyed eating during school recess. Always hot, it was always a hit even though the vendors were stingy on the delicious stuffing. So, stuff your dough à go-go! You deserve it!

YOU WILL NEED

For the dough

- 1.5 cups of flour
- 1 egg
- 1 teaspoon of sugar
- 3 tablespoons of water
- 1 tablespoon of olive oil
- ½ a teaspoon of Kosher salt
- ½ a teaspoon of yeast

For the stuffing

- 1 can of tuna or 1 fish (any type) without bones
- 1 onion
- 2 - 3 cloves of garlic
- Diced tomatoes
- Salt and pepper to taste
- 2 tablespoons of water
- 1 habanero pepper
- 1 beaten egg

PROCEDURE

- Mix the yeast to the water, add the tablespoon of sugar and let it rise and foam.
- Then, add salt and oil to flour and mix well. Next, add the foamy yeast mixture to the flour and mix-knead for 5 minutes.
- Cover the dough and set it aside for at least an hour.
- Sautéed the fish, diced onions, garlic, tomatoes, and pepper. Add the water, stir and let it cook a bit.
- Season the sauce with salt and pepper to taste and let it simmer more until ready or cooked to your taste. Approximately 5 - 10 minutes.
- Then, divide the dough in equal portions and flatten them into uneven circles with a rolling pin.
- Put the stuffing in the flattened dough and close with your fingers.
- Deep fry at medium heat and remove when cooked and brown.

GBOFLOTOS OR GALETTES AU SUCRE

Beignets

(Serves 1-4)

TOP INSIGHT

Gboflotos or Beignets are quite universal. Every day, you're sure to smell their aroma in the streets of Ivory Coast. Only the shape differs in Ivory Coast. That being said, they are very reminiscent of doughnut balls or holes. Gboflotos also taste great with Ivorian café. Thus, it's also a breakfast meal and it reminds us of the customary American favorite; coffee and donuts.

YOU WILL NEED

- 2 cups of flour
- 2 tablespoons of sugar
- 1.5 cups of hot water
- 1 packet of vanillin sugar
- 1 tablespoon of olive oil
- ½ a teaspoon of Kosher salt
- 1 teaspoon of yeast
- 1 liter of frying oil
- Additional granulated sugar for garnish

PROCEDURE

- Mix the yeast to the water, add the tablespoon of sugar and let it rise and foam.
- Then, add salt, vanillin sugar and oil to flour and mix well.
- Next, add the foamy yeast mixture to the flour and whip it well for 5 for 15 minutes.
- Cover the dough and set it aside for at least 1 to 2 hours.
- After the time elapses, with a spoon or your right hand, drop dollops of the paste into the heated deep fryer.
- Keep doing this until your whole mixture is finished.
- Fry on medium heat until they turn browny red and remove to set aside.
- Garnish with sugar serve.

TRA-TRA

Fried Nutmeg Dough

(Serves 1-4)

TOP INSIGHT

Tra-Tra (Tratra) was always Feauxzar's favorite beignets since her toddler years. These beignets are flavorful, flat and a bit sweet. These pancakes also look like Russian Curd Fritters if you put less nutmeg in the Tratra dough. Try them.

YOU WILL NEED

- 1.5 cups of flour
- 3 tablespoons of sugar
- 1 cup of hot water
- 1 packet of vanillin sugar
- 1 teaspoon of nutmeg
- 1 tablespoon of olive oil
- ½ a teaspoon of Kosher salt
- 1 tablespoon of yeast
- ¼ of liter of frying oil

PROCEDURE

- Mix the yeast to the water, add 1 tablespoon of sugar and let it rise and foam.
- Then, add salt, nutmeg, remaining tablespoons of sugar and oil to the flour and mix well. Next, add the foamy yeast mixture to the flour and mix-knead for 5 minutes.
- Cover the dough and set it aside for at least 4 hours.
- After the time elapses, with a spoon or your right hand, drop dollops of the paste into the heated omelet pan. Keep doing this until your whole mixture is finished.
- Tip*: this snack is not deep-fried. You only need a little bit of oil to cook each side. When you flip one cooked side of the dough, press the spatula to flatten the dough.
- Cook on medium heat until they turn browny red and remove to set aside.

ALLER-RETOUR OR GALETTE JAUNE-JAUNE À LA VERMICELLE

Yellow Fried Dough

(Serves 1-3)

TOP INSIGHT

Aller-Retour is a naturally colored fried dough. It's very enjoyed during school recess. The vermicelli enhances the taste.

YOU WILL NEED

- 1 cup of flour
- 1 tablespoon of sugar
- ½ a cup of hot water
- 1 tablespoons of olive oil
- ½ a teaspoon of Kosher salt
- 1 tablespoon of yeast
- 1 liter of frying oil
- 1 teaspoon of turmeric for coloring
- 1 pack of vermicelli
- 1 onion
- 3 cloves of garlic
- 1.5 cups of diced tomatoes
- 3 diced green onions
- Salt and pepper to taste

PROCEDURE

- Mix the yeast to the water, add the tablespoon of sugar and let it rise and foam. Then, add salt, turmeric and oil to flour and mix well. Next, add the foamy yeast mixture to the flour and mix-knead for 5 minutes.
- Cover the dough and set it aside for at least 3 - 4 hours. After the time elapses, with a spoon or your right hand, drop dollops of the paste into the heated deep fryer. Keep doing this until your whole mixture is finished. Fry on medium heat until they turn browny red and remove to set aside. Sautéed diced onions, garlic, tomatoes, and green onions. Season the sauce with salt and pepper to taste and let it simmer until ready or cooked to your taste. Approximately 5 - 10 minutes. Boil vermicelli with salty water and mix to the sauce above. Serve the Aller-Retour with the vermicelli. Enjoy!

PASTELS DE POISSON

Half-moon Beignets with Fish

(Serves 1-3)

TOP INSIGHT

Pastels are almost found in any culture. The stuffing is cheese or meat in Turkey. In Brazil, it's often meat. In Ivory Coast, it's always fish stuffing. Hello, the ocean is right there!

YOU WILL NEED

For the dough

- 1.5 cups of flour
- 1 egg
- 1 teaspoon of sugar
- 3 tablespoons of water
- 1 tablespoon of olive oil
- ½ a teaspoon of Kosher salt
- ½ a teaspoon of yeast

For the stuffing

- 1 can of tuna or 1 fish (any type) without bones
- 1 onion
- 2 - 3 cloves of garlic
- diced tomato
- Salt and pepper to taste
- tablespoons of water
- 1 habanero pepper
- 1 beaten egg

PROCEDURE

- Mix the yeast to the water, add the tablespoon of sugar and let it rise and foam.
- Then, add salt and oil to flour and mix well. Next, add the foamy yeast mixture to the flour and mix-knead for 5 minutes.
- Cover the dough and set it aside for at least an hour.
- Sautéed the fish, diced onions, garlic, tomatoes, and pepper. Add the water, stir and let it cook a bit.
- Season the sauce with salt and pepper to taste and let it simmer more until ready or cooked to your taste. Approximately 5 - 10 minutes.
- Then, divide the dough in equal portions and flatten them into circles with a rolling pin.
- Put the stuffing in the flattened dough and close the tips by pressing a fork along the edges.
- Brush the top of the pastels with an egg wash.
- Fry at medium heat and remove when cooked and golden. Serve and enjoy.

KRÉKRÉ

Dried Breadsticks

(Serves 1-3)

TOP INSIGHT

Krékré are a type of dried breadsticks; Grissini (Italian Breadsticks.) The difference is that the Ivorian kind is circle-shaped and browner. Sometimes, there are salty or a bit sweet. The circle of breadstick is broken into pieces to eat.

YOU WILL NEED

- 2 cups of flour
- 1 cup of warm water
- 1 teaspoon of salt
- 1 tablespoon of yeast
- 1 liter of frying oil
- ¼ of a cup of sugar
- 1 tablespoon of sugar

PROCEDURE

- Mix the yeast to the water, add the tablespoon of sugar and let it rise and foam.
- Then, add the foamy mixture to the flour and mix-knead for 5 minutes. Cover the dough and set it aside for at least an hour.
- Then, divide the dough in equal portions and roll them into ropes like you would with a regular pretzel. Connect the tips of the ropes to make a necklace. Do this until all pieces have been transformed into dough necklaces. Now, fry them on medium heat until brown and cooked.
- Enjoy!

STEWS & ENTRÉES

"I love Yam Patties because the dish reminds me of my sweet grandmother. When I was a child, she often ate that dish and fed it to us too."— Haby bint Mamadou Karamoko

SAUCE GRAINE

Palm Nut Stew

(Serves 4-6)

YOU WILL NEED

- 1 can of palm nut paste
- 1 onion
- 3 cloves of garlic
- 1 tomato
- Salt and pepper to taste
- 1 teaspoon of tomato paste
- 1 tablespoon of olive oil (optional)
- 1 habanero pepper
- 4 to 8 glasses of water
- ½ a pound of fresh cleaned meat

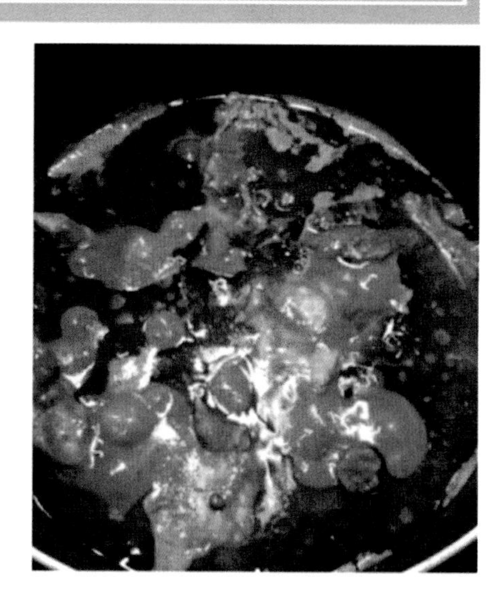

PROCEDURE

- Put the fresh meat in a pan and add the garlic, salt, pepper, 2 - 3 glasses of water and let the meat cook until tender.
- Then, add the olive oil, the diced onions, tomato and paste to the pot of meat to be sautéed.
- Add 2 - 3 glasses of water, the palm nut paste, and the habanero pepper.
- Let the mélange cook for 30 - 40 minutes at medium heat.
- Tip*: You can add a glass of water to the palm nut paste and filter it before cooking if you fear it may contain rocks or debris from the shells of the palm nut.
- Add salt and pepper and wait another 5 minutes to turn off the heat.
- Tip*: Adding dried shrimp and fish powders are optional with African stews. So if you have food allergies or religious food restrictions, you can still enjoy these stews your way.
- Serve with rice or foutou.

TOP INSIGHT

Sauce Graine is often served with rice along with foutou banane (mashed plantain banana patties.) The stew is creamy and rich. Leftovers of this stew and rice make the best riz couché. Find the method on page 10. O n a side note, African stews are often called a zoo jokingly because they always contain an array of meat. For instance, you will often find *kpolo* (cooked beef skin without the hair), crabs, smoked and fresh meats all in the same stew at times.

FOUTOU BANANE

Plantain Banana Patties

(Serves 5-10)

YOU WILL NEED

- 1 - 3 plantain bananas
- 1 cassava root
- ½ a liter of water. Or
- 2 cups of plantain flour. Add more if needed.
- 1 - 2 ripe plantain bananas
- 2.5 cups of water

PROCEDURE

- Peel the bananas and the cassavas, gut and wash them. In a good size pot, place the cassava first at the bottom and then add the plantain at the top. Add the water and boil for 20 - 30 minutes.
- Pound the cassava until it's completely uniform and mashed. Remove it and pound the plantain now. When both are mashed and uniform, mix them by pounding them more.
- Mold them into small patties and put them in a serving dish.

Or

- Peel the bananas, gut and wash them. Boil the bananas with 1 cup of water and mash/blend them. In another pot, mix 1.5 cups of water to the plantain flour.
- When the mixture is uniform, cook it at low heat and whip it regularly with a spatula. Fold in the puree of ripe bananas until it is a blended mixture. Also mold them into small patties and put them in a serving dish. Eat with a stew of your liking. Sauce Graine is preferred.

TOP INSIGHT

Foutou Banane is a mashed and pounded tube that is filling, delicious, and festive. You can make it plain or add some pounded yams or cassava to it. You will need some muscles and a small mortar and pestle.

EXTRAS

Foutou Banane avec du Riz

(Serves 1 - 2)

TOP INSIGHT

Foutou Banane is often served with rice, a stew and a soup. The soup is usually mixed to the stew in order to be consumed with the rice and the foutou. See below. From top the right to the left of the page: Fish soup, dried okra soup, plantain patty (Foufou*) and rice.

*Foufou: requires adding some palm nut oil and a little salt to the boiled and pounded banana. No other tube such as yams or cassava is added to it.

FOUTOU IGNAME

Yam Patties

(Serves 1-2)

YOU WILL NEED

- 1 fresh yam
- ½ a liter of water or
- 2 cups of yam flour. Add more if needed.
- 1 cup of water

PROCEDURE

- Peel the yams and wash them.
- In a good size pot, place the yams, add the water and boil for 10 - 30 minutes.
- Tip*: If the yams are really fresh, the water doesn't need to cover them. They will cook rather quickly. However, if the yams are old, they will need more water to be cooked.
- Pound the cooked yams until it's completely uniform, mashed, and a bit elastic.
- Mold them into small patties and put them in a serving dish.

Or

- In another pot, mix 1 cup of water to the plantain flour. When the mixture is uniform, cook it at low heat and whip it regularly with a spatula.
- Also mold them into small patties and put them in a serving dish.
- Eat with a stew of your liking. Sauce Arachide on page 74 is preferred.

TOP INSIGHT

Foutou Igname is reminiscent of mashed potatoes. The difference is that it's thicker and more elastic than potatoes. You will need some muscles and a small mortar and pestle here too.

SAUCE DJOUMBLÉ

Dried Tiny Okra Stew

(Serves 1-3)

YOU WILL NEED

- 1 - 4 tablespoons of powdered djoumblé
- 1 onion
- 1 clove of garlic
- 2 diced tomatoes
- ¼ of a cup of olive oil
- 2- 4 tablespoons of palm nut oil
- Salt and pepper to taste
- 1 habanero pepper
- Water
- Some smoked fish, fresh cleaned fish, fresh cleaned meat or clean smoked meat

PROCEDURE

- Put the fresh meat and smoked meat in a pan and add the garlic, salt, pepper, 2 - 3 glasses of water and let the meat cook until tender.
- Wash the smoked fish and crumbed it into big pieces removing anything that shouldn't be in it such as sand, fish's feces and gills.
- Then, add the olive oil, the diced onions, tomato and paste to the pot of meat to be sautéed. Add 2 - 3 glasses of water, the palm nut oil, the habanero pepper and the fishes.
- Let the mélange cook for 15 - 20 mins.
- Add a tablespoon or two of water to the powder and djoumblé and mix well.
- Transfer, the mixture to the pot and stir.
- Add salt and pepper and wait another 5 minutes to turn off the heat.
- Serve with rice or foutou.

TOP INSIGHT

Sauce Djoumblé is a type of okra stew. The okra is dried and blended into a powder. The powder of this type of okra is black. It's different from dried and fresh okra whose dried powder is still green. Both types of okra taste great when added into Sauce Graine; especially the Djoumblé powder. It gives it a gooey and rich taste.

DJÉ NAN OR SAUCE DE COURGE

Butternut Squash Stew

(Serves 1-3)

YOU WILL NEED

- 1 butternut squash
- 1 onion
- 1 clove of garlic
- 2 diced tomatoes
- ¼ of a cup of olive oil
- Salt and pepper to taste
- 1 teaspoon of tomato paste
- 1 habanero pepper
- Water
- Boiled and pre-cooked fresh meat.
- Tip*: Pre-cooking and freezing fresh meat is a great time saver when it comes to making African stews and other dishes.

PROCEDURE

- In a pan add the defrosted boiled and pre-cooked fresh meat, the garlic, salt, olive oil, diced onions, tomato and paste to the pot of meat to be sautéed. Add 2 - 3 glasses of water and bring them to boil at medium heat.
- Gut and wash the squash.
- Tip*: the seeds of a butternut squash are used to make Sauce Pistache. Pistache is also different than Pistachio. So, perhaps harness the seeds for later use if not baking them like peanuts to eat as a snack.
- Cut and add it to the boiling stew to cook it. Let the mélange cook for 15 - 20 mins or until the squash is soft and cooked.
- Remove the squash and blend in a food processor or in a mortar and pestle.
- Add the squash paste back into the stew and lower the heat.
- Add salt and pepper and wait another 5 minutes to turn off the heat. Serve with rice or eat as a soup.

TOP INSIGHT

Djé Nan is very creamy and has a sweet zucchini's stew taste. You have to try it!

KÉDJÉNOU DE POULET

Spicy Chicken Stew

(Serves 5-6)

YOU WILL NEED

- 1 whole chicken cut into pieces. A guinea fowl or escargots will work too.
- 1 large diced onion
- 3 clove of garlics
- 2 diced tomatoes plus 1 tablespoon of tomato paste. Mix them well.
- 1 diced eggplant
- 1/2 a cup of olive oil
- Salt and pepper to taste
- 1 - 2 habanero peppers
- 1 smashed ginger root
- 1 teaspoon of paprika
- 2 bay leaves
- 1 small bunch of chopped green onions
- 1 small bunch of chopped parsley

PROCEDURE

- In the canari shape cooking pot or Dutch oven, place the chicken first at the bottom.
- Then add the olive oil and all the vegetable ingredients.
- Next, add the salt and pepper last.
- Cover with some aluminium paper.
- Cook on low heat for 45 to 90 minutes.

TOP INSIGHT

Kédjénou means 'shaking the insides' in Baoulé; a tribe from the Akans ethnic group of Ivory Coast. The dish is normally cooked in a clay pot called *canari*. The *canari* is tightly covered with banana leaves to enhance the taste of the stew by simmering and slow cooking. The closest pan wares you can buy overseas to make this stew are crock pots and Dutch ovens. While the dish is cooking, it is not stirred with a spatula, spoon or any other utensil. Only the WHOLE pot is stirred every fifteen minutes with two hands to prevent the stew to burn or the chicken to stick to the bottom of the canari or Dutch oven. Kédjénou is served with rice or attiéké. So check out the recipe with a unique aroma.

SAUCE ARACHIDE

Peanut Butter Stew

(Serves 2-4)

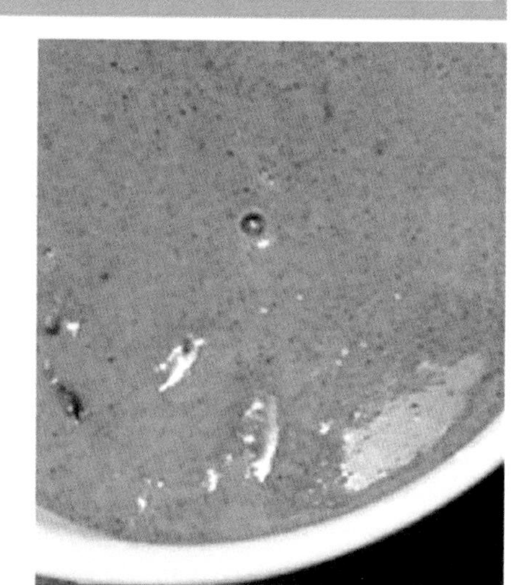

YOU WILL NEED

- 1 small jar of peanut butter
- 1 onion
- 1 clove of garlic
- 2 diced tomatoes
- Salt and black pepper to taste
- 1 teaspoon of tomato paste
- 1 habanero pepper
- Water
- Boiled and pre-cooked fresh meat. Lamb meat is preferred.
- 1/4 to 1/2 cup of *Ndah* leaves—Sorrel leaves (optional)
- Tip*: Pre-cooking and freezing fresh meat is a great time saver when it comes to making African stews and other dishes.

PROCEDURE

- In a cooking pan, add the defrosted boiled and pre-cooked fresh meat, the garlic, salt, black pepper, diced onions, tomatoes and paste to the pot of meat to be stir-fried at medium heat.
- Add the peanut butter and continue stir-frying rapidly until the butter changes color and starts emitting oil. Be vigilant so that it doesn't burn.
- Add 2 - 3 glasses of water and bring them to boil at medium heat. Add the habanero pepper and *Ndah* leaves once the stew starts boiling. Then, let the stew cook for 15 - 40 mins or until the stew thickens.
- Add salt and pepper and wait another 5 minutes to turn off the heat. Serve with rice or Foutou Igname.

TOP INSIGHT

Sauce Arachide is perhaps the first dish that is easily eaten by people from other cultures; especially Americans. Peanut butter is something that they already enjoy eating. So, it's an acquired taste to them.

Fry your peanut butter as prescribed in this recipe. If you just put some water in peanut butter to get a uniform liquid and add it at boiling point, the taste is less than stellar. Trust us, pre-fried peanut butter and boiled peanut butter stews taste outlandishly different! Much like Sauce Graine, oil is optional in this stew. Boiled spinach can be added to peanut butter stew. It's definitely optional. As final insight, Peanut Butter Stew with lamb is a customary dish for *eid* (The two religious holidays for Muslims.)

Peanut Butter Stew with Rice

Peanut Butter Stew with Sweet Pounded Yams

SAUCE FEUILLE (ÉPINARD, MANIOC OU TARO)

Spinach, Cassava or Taro Leaves Stews

(Serves 2-4)

YOU WILL NEED

- 1 frozen bag of cassava or spinach leaves
- 1 onion
- 1 clove of garlic
- 2 diced tomatoes
- ¼ of a cup of olive oil (optional)
- ½ a cup of palm nut oil (optional)
- Salt and pepper to taste
- 1 teaspoon of tomato paste
- 1 habanero pepper
- ½ of peanut butter for the cassava stew (optional)
- Water
- Boiled and pre-cooked fresh meat.
- Tip*: Pre-cooking and freezing fresh meat is a great time saver when it comes to making African stews and other dishes.

PROCEDURE

- In a pan add the defrosted boiled and pre-cooked fresh meat, the garlic, salt, olive oil, diced onions, tomato and paste to the pot of meat to be sautéed.
- Add 2 - 3 glasses of water and bring them to boil at medium heat.
- Add the leaves desired to the boiling stew to cook them.
- Tip*: If you're using fresh leaves, wash and boil them ahead of time and adjust the cooking time accordingly.
- Let the mélange cook for 15 - 20 mins. Then add the palm nut oil.
- Tip*: Palm nut oil is optional for spinach stew.
- Add salt and pepper and wait another 5 minutes to turn off the heat. Serve with rice.

TOP INSIGHT

There are more vegetable leaves to make stews from in Ivory Coast but these three are the ones we often used in our home.
Taro leaves were mostly used for an Indian dish with a curry paste. Thanks to an Indian family friend who taught us to use it this way too.
And talking about leaves, Ivorians do eat salads; the most popular one being romaine lettuce. We won't cover them in this book.

PLACALI

Cassava Fufu

(Serves 2-4)

YOU WILL NEED

- 1 frozen bag of cassava paste.
- 2 liters of water

PROCEDURE

- In a large container pot, mix 1 liter of water to the cassava paste. Let it sit for ½ - 1 hour. The paste will go to the bottom and the water will stay at the top. Delicately remove the water and put the wet cassava paste in the cooking pan. Cook it at low heat and whip it regularly with a spatula.
- The paste will start to harden. Continue whipping it with a spatula until it becomes opaque. Add ½ a cup of water to it and then, lower the heat. Let it steam for 5 - 15 minutes.
- When cooked, dip a ladle in water and then put it back into the placali.
- Transfer the placali into a service plate by taking large spoonfuls of it. Continue doing this until you remove all the placali from the cooking pot. The serving dish should be filled with small patties now.
- Eat with a stew of your liking. Sauce Kplala or Djoumblé are preferred.

TOP INSIGHT

Placali is made from the fresh paste of cassava also known as yucca root. It's scrumptiously a bit sour. See below a picture of placali with a highly inventive stew not usually consumed with placali! But that's what you do when you leave home; you become too crafty when you're lacking original ingredients. Placali's leftovers also make a great breakfast much like Tô on page 93.

SAUCE KPLALA

Molokhia Stew

(Serves 1-2)

YOU WILL NEED

- 1 frozen bag of Kplala (Molokhia) leaves. Use the whole bag if you want a completely green sauce. In **Fofky's Kitchen**, we use Kplala sparingly such as a cup of leaves of less.
- 1 liter of water
- Tip*: Adding dried shrimp and fish powders are optional with African stews.
- Buy your meat of preference.
- Tip*: Crabs, dried and smoked fishes are preferred in Ivory Coast. There are also optional.
- Dried or fresh Ivorian mushrooms; black and white types
- 1 small rock of *potasse* salt
- 1 small *adjovan* (fermented fish) piece
- 1 - 2 habanero peppers
- 1 liter of water
- Salt and pepper to taste
- 1 onion
- 4 cloves of garlic
- 1 tomato plus a teaspoon of tomato paste

PROCEDURE

- In a pan add the defrosted boiled and pre-cooked fresh meat and others, the garlic, salt, olive oil, diced onions, tomato and paste to the pot of meat to be sautéed.
- Add 2 - 3 glasses of water, the washed *adjovan* and bring them to boil at medium heat.
- When it boils, add the leaves, *potasse*, habanero peppers to the boiling stew to cook them.
- Tip*: The *potasse* helps the leaves stay sticky.
- Tip*: And if you're using fresh leaves, wash and boil them ahead of time and adjust the cooking time accordingly.
- Let the *mélange* cook for 15 - 20 mins. Then, add the palm nut oil.
- Add salt and pepper and wait another 5 minutes to turn off the heat.
- Serve with foutou, placali and/or rice.

TOP INSIGHT

Molokhia has a consistency and taste similar to okra. However, it's a bit bitter. It has numerous health benefits and a special spot at African and Ivorian tables.

EXTRAS

Mushrooms

(Black & White)

TOP INSIGHT

Here is another fun fact; sometimes, mushrooms are added in stews in lieu of meat. Check out some black and white mushrooms used in Ivory Coast depicted on this page.

SOUPE DE POISSON

Fish Soup

(Serves 1-2)

YOU WILL NEED

- 1 fresh or dry Mâchoiron (Catfish) or any other fish such as a carp
- 1 - 2 habanero peppers
- 1 liter of water
- Salt and pepper to taste
- 1 onion
- 3 cloves of garlic
- 2 tomatoes plus a teaspoon of tomato paste
- 1 small bunch of diced green onions

PROCEDURE

- In a pan add the garlic, salt, olive oil, diced onions, tomatoes and paste to the pot. Sauté for 5 - 10 mins.
- Next, add 2 - 3 glasses of water and bring them to boil at medium heat.
- When the water starts boiling, add the habanero pepper and the washed and cleaned fish. Let them cook for 20 to 30 minutes at low to medium heat.
- Then, add salt and pepper and wait another 5 minutes to turn off the heat.
- Serve with attiéké or rice. You can also savor it with bread.

TOP INSIGHT

Fish Soup is also enjoyed when one feels under the weather. In this case, some mashed bitter African eggplants are added to the soup.

SOUPE DE TÊTE DE MOUTTON

Lamb Head Stew

(Serves 1-2)

YOU WILL NEED

- 1 head of lamb cut and cleaned
- 1 - 2 habanero peppers
- 1 liter of water
- Salt and pepper to taste
- 1 onion
- 2 cloves of garlic
- 2 tomatoes
- 1 teaspoon of tomato paste
- 1 small bunch of diced green onions
- 1 teaspoon of dried fish (optional)
- 1 teaspoon of dried shrimp (optional

PROCEDURE

- In a pan, add the defrosted boiled and pre-cooked meat. Then, add the garlic, salt, olive oil, diced onions, tomatoes and paste to the pot. Sauté for 5 - 10 mins.
- Next, add 2 - 3 glasses of water and bring them to boil at medium heat. When the water starts boiling add the habanero peppers.
- Let them cook for 20 to 30 minutes.
- Then, add salt and pepper and wait another 5 minutes to turn off the heat.
- Also add the dried seafood if using.
- Serve with bread, *attiéké* or rice.

TOP INSIGHT

Africans in general like to suck on bones. This is a perfect soup for that. Lamb head stew is popular during *eid*.

SOUPE DE TRIPE DE MOUTON

Lamb Intestine Soup

(Serves 1-2)

YOU WILL NEED

- ½ a pound of washed and cleaned lamb intestine
- 1 - 2 habanero peppers
- 1 liter of water
- Salt and pepper to taste
- 1 onion
- 1 clove of garlic
- 2 tomatoes
- 1 teaspoon of tomato paste
- 1 small bunch of diced green onions
- 1 small bunch of chopped parsley

PROCEDURE

- In a pan, add the defrosted boiled and pre-cooked intestine meat.
- Sautée for 5 - 10 mins.
- Then, add the garlic, salt, olive oil, chopped parsley, diced onions, tomatoes and paste to the pot to be sautéed for 5 - 10 mins.
- Add 2 - 3 glasses of water and bring them to boil at medium heat.
- When the water starts boiling, add the habanero peppers. Let them cook for 20 to 30 minutes.
- Then, add salt and pepper and wait another 5 minutes to turn off the heat.
- Serve with bread, *attiéké* or rice.

TOP INSIGHT

Lamb Intestine Soup is also popular during *eid*. After the hard job that is cleaning it meticulously, it's wonderful to enjoy the food bliss one it's cooked and spiced up.

SAUCE AUBERGINE

Garden Eggplant Stew

(Serves 1-2)

YOU WILL NEED

- ½ a pound of pre-cooked meat
- 1 - 2 habanero peppers
- 1 liter of water
- 5-10 garden egg eggplants
- Salt and pepper to taste
- 1 onion
- 1 clove of garlic
- 2 tomatoes
- 1 teaspoon of tomato paste
- 1 small bunch of diced green onions
- 1 teaspoon of dried fish (optional)
- 1 teaspoon of dried shrimp (optional)
- 2 - 3 ***apki**** toasted and pounded to a powder/paste

PROCEDURE

- In a pan, add the defrosted boiled and pre-cooked meat. Then, add the garlic, salt, olive oil, diced onions, tomatoes and paste to the pot. Sautée for 5 - 10 mins.
- Next, add 2 - 3 glasses of water and bring them to boil at medium heat.
- When the water starts boiling, add the eggplants, *apki*, habanero peppers and the washed and cleaned meat.
- Let them cook for 15 to 30 minutes.
- Remove them and mash them before the returning the mashed eggplants back to the stew. Add more water and the dried seafood if using. Stir, add some salt and pepper and wait another 10 - 15 minutes to turn off the heat.
- Serve with attiéké, attoukou, or rice.

SAUCE DE GNANGNAN

Bitter African Eggplant Soup

(Serves 2-4)

YOU WILL NEED

- ½ a pound of pre-cooked meat
- 1 smoked fish
- 1 habanero pepper
- 1 liter of water
- 1 handful of bitter eggplant
- Salt and pepper to taste
- 1 onion & 1 clove of garlic
- 2 tomatoes plus a teaspoon of tomato paste
- 1 small bunch of diced green onions
- 1 teaspoon of dried fish (optional)
- 1 teaspoon of dried shrimp (optional)

PROCEDURE

- In a pan, add the defrosted boiled and pre-cooked meat. Then, add the garlic, salt, olive oil, diced onions, tomatoes and paste to the pot. Sauté for 5 - 10 mins. Next, add 2 - 3 glasses of water and bring them to boil at medium heat. When the water starts boiling, add the gnangnan, and habanero pepper.
- Tip*: You can also use ¼-1/2 of a cup of frozen gnangnan. Remember, they are bitter.
- Let them cook for 15 to 30 minutes.
- Remove them and mash them before the returning the mashed eggplants back to the stew. Add more water and the dried seafood if using. Stir, add some salt and pepper and wait another 10 - 15 minutes to turn off the heat.

TOP INSIGHT

Gnangnan has a lot of healing properties. Many people dry it and add the powder to every dish they eat. Others only eat it occasionally. It's up to you how to use it.

ZRAMIN OR RIZ GRAS

Greasy Rice or Seasoned Rice with Tomato Sauce

(Serves 4-8)

YOU WILL NEED

- ½ - 1 pound of pre-cooked meat (Chicken preferred.)
- 4 cups of rice
- 1 liter of water
- Salt and pepper to taste
- 1 large diced onion
- 4 tomatoes
- 5 tablespoons of tomato paste
- 1 small bunch of diced green onions
- 1 small bunch of chopped parsley
- 3 - 5 cloves of garlic
- 1 cup of olive oil
- ½ a cabbage cut in several pieces (optional)
- 1 cassava root (optional)
- 2 carrots cut in six pieces or less (optional)
- 1 purple eggplant (optional)
- 1 small bunch of boiled *Ndah* sour leaves (optional)

PROCEDURE

- In a pan, add the defrosted boiled and pre-cooked meat.
- Then, add the garlic, salt, olive oil, chopped parsley, diced onions, tomatoes and tomato paste to the pot.
- Stir fry until the sauce looks sautéed.
- Add the washed and air-dried rice. Continue stirring so that the mix doesn't burn. When the rice starts to looks translucent, add the gutted/cut cassava, habanero pepper, cut purple eggplant, carrots and cabbage pieces.
- Next, add the water and bring them to boil at medium heat. Once all the water evaporates, taste it to see if it needs some additional seasoning such as salt and pepper. If so, add more seasoning to taste.
- Then lower the heat and let the rice cook for 15 to 30 minutes to steam-cook.
- When the time elapses, the rice should red, very moist, and well-seasoned.
- Turn off the heat. Serve and eat. Refrigerate any remaining food.

TOP INSIGHT

Riz Gras is an Ivorian favorite. It's simply festive and rich taste wise. While many of the ingredients are optional, cassava, eggplant and *ndah* (feuilles d' *oseille* or sorrel leaves) enhance its taste in our opinion. A *soumara* sauce is also an optional side dish here. Some spices such as dry fish and shrimp, salt, pepper and oil are added to it to season and cook a bit.

LAFRI - RIZ PERDU

Seasoned Rice with Néré Seeds

(Serves 2-4)

YOU WILL NEED

- 4 cups of rice
- 1 liter of water
- 2 teaspoons of powdered *soumara*
- Salt and pepper to taste
- 2 cups of palm nut oil (optional)
- 1 large diced onion
- 1 tomato plus 1 teaspoon of tomato paste
- 1 small bunch of chopped green onions
- 2 cloves of diced garlic
- 3 - 5 garden egg eggplants
- 3 - 5 okras
- 1 habanero pepper
- 1 teaspoon of dried fish (optional)
- 1 teaspoon of dried shrimp (optional)

PROCEDURE

- In a pan, add 1 cup of palm nut oil, 1 teaspoon of *soumara*, the garlic, salt, chopped and diced onions, tomatoes and tomato paste to the pot.
- Stir fry until the sauce looks sautéed. Next, add the water and bring them to boil at medium heat.
- At boiling point, add the okras, eggplants, and peppers. Cook the soup for 10 to 15 minutes to allow the vegetables to cook. Once cooked, remove and set them aside.
- Add the washed and air-dried rice to the soup. Add more salt, pepper and garlic if needed.
- Once all the water evaporates and that the rice is softer, make a whole in the rice and insert the remaining *soumara* along with the dried fish and shrimp. Cover it back up and close the pot to let it steam. Then, lower the heat and let the rice cook for 15 to 30 minutes to cook. When the time elapses, dump the rice in a large container and mix it.
- Add the remaining cup of palm nut oil if using palm nut.
- Garnish with the okra, pepper, and eggplant.
- Serve and eat. Refrigerate any remainder.

TOP INSIGHT

Lafri is a dish that is very popular in the west coast of Ivory Coast; most precisely the region of Man. It's made with *soumara (soumbala)* also known as néré seeds. *Soumara* has a very pungent smell but it tastes great once fully cooked. From experience, don't cook this dish around anyone who isn't familiar with the smell. They will flip and try to call the police on you because of the smell! It's aggressive to the senses. It happened to a family relative. The diplomatic ordeal was hilarious after the fact. So, you've been warned! Depending on whether you omit the palm oil or not, your rice will be either light brown or orange tinted.

GBAN NAN OR SAUCE DE GOMBO FRAIS

Fresh Okra Stew

(Serves 2-4)

YOU WILL NEED

- 1 bag of frozen and uncooked diced okra
- ½ a liter of water
- Salt and pepper to taste
- 1 small rock of *potasse* salt to prevent losing the unique texture of okra.

PROCEDURE

- In a pan, add the water, *potasse*, salt and pepper.
- When the water starts boiling, add the defrosted okra.
- Let them cook open for 10 - 15 minutes.
- Once, it starts boiling, whip it with wooden spoon. You will know the okra is ready when the seeds are turning a light purple shade.
- So turn off the heat.

TOP INSIGHT

Gban Nan is best eaten with Foutou or Tô (Cornmeal Patty on page 93) along with a protein stew.

Tip*: Okra promotes hair growth.

GBANMROU NAN OR
SAUCE DE GOMBO FRAIS SEC

Dried Fresh Okra Stew

(Serves 1-2)

YOU WILL NEED

- 1 - 4 tablespoons of *gbanmrou* (dry fresh okra powder)
- 1 onion
- 1 clove of garlic
- 2 diced tomatoes plus 1 teaspoon of tomato paste
- ¼ of a cup of olive oil
- 2- 4 tablespoons of palm nut oil
- Salt and pepper to taste
- 1 habanero pepper
- Water
- Some smoked fish, fresh cleaned fish, fresh cleaned meat or clean smoked meat
- 1 teaspoon of dried fish powder (optional)
- 1 teaspoon of dried shrimp powder (optional)

PROCEDURE

- Put the fresh meat and smoked meat in a pan and add the garlic, salt, pepper, 2 - 3 glasses of water and let the meat cook until tender.
- Wash the smoked fish and crumbed it into big pieces removing anything that shouldn't be in it such as sand, fish's feces and gills.
- Then, add the olive oil, the diced onions, tomato and paste to the pot of meat to be sautéed.
- Add 2 - 3 glasses of water, the palm nut oil, the habanero pepper and the fishes. Let the mélange cook for 15 - 20 mins.
- Add a tablespoon or two of water to the powder and gbanmrou and mix well. Transfer, the mixture to the pot and stir.
- Add salt and pepper. Also add the dried seafood if using. Wait another 5 minutes to turn off the heat.
- Serve with rice or *foutou*.

SAUCE DE PISTACHE OR SAUCE DE GRAIN DE COURGES

Butternut Squash's Seed Stew

(Serves 2-4)

YOU WILL NEED

- Pistache butter from at least 2 squashes
- 1 onion
- Juice from 1 smashed ginger root
- 1 clove of garlic
- 2 diced tomatoes
- Salt and black pepper to taste
- 1 teaspoon of tomato paste
- 1 habanero pepper
- Water
- Boiled and pre-cooked fresh meat. Chicken meat is preferred.

PROCEDURE

- In a cooking pan, add the defrosted boiled and pre-cooked fresh meat, the garlic, salt, black pepper, diced onions, tomatoes and paste to the pot of meat to be stir-fried at medium heat.
- Add the squash butter and continue stir-frying rapidly until the butter changes color and starts emitting oil. Be vigilant so that it doesn't burn.
- Add 2 - 3 glasses of water and bring them to boil at medium heat.
- Add the habanero pepper once the stew starts boiling. Then, let the stew cook for 15 - 40 mins or until the stew thickens.
- Add salt and pepper and wait another 5 minutes to turn off the heat.
- Serve with rice or Foutou Igname.

TOP INSIGHT

Sauce Pistache is made with the butter of Butternut Squash's seeds. We used to make this butter along with peanut butter from scratch in our teen years. Both Pistache and Peanut have the same process if one wants to harness their butter. The seeds just need to be roasted for 10 to 15 minutes on medium heat and then pounded. Then, they are further processed with a rolling pin to make them creamy and buttery. Back then, we used an oily glass bottle as rolling pin. To save you from all this work, just toast them in an omelet pan and then dump them into a food processor for further blending. Add some water and use the hand blender to blend the mixture. It will look like the color of watered peanut butter.

HARICOT ROUGE

Red Beans

(Serves 2-3)

YOU WILL NEED

- 2 cups of red beans
- 1 onion
- 1 clove of garlic
- 2 diced tomatoes
- Salt and black pepper to taste
- 1 teaspoon of tomato paste
- 1 teaspoon of paprika
- 1 teaspoon of cayenne or ground red pepper
- 1 small rock of *potasse* salt
- Water
- Boiled and pre-cooked fresh meat.

PROCEDURE

- Wash and boil the beans with the *potasse* for 20 to 60 minutes. The *potasse* will make it cook faster.
- In another cooking pan, add the defrosted boiled and pre-cooked fresh meat, the garlic, salt, black pepper, diced onions, tomatoes and paste to the pot of meat to be stir-fried at medium heat.
- Add 2 - 3 glasses of water and bring them to boil at medium heat.
- Add the cooked beans, cayenne pepper once the stew starts boiling.
- Then, let the stew cook for 15 - 40 mins or until the stew thickens.
- Add salt, paprika and pepper and wait another 5 minutes to turn off the heat.
- Serve with rice if needed. In Burkina Faso, red beans and boiled white rice is a local dish.

TOP INSIGHT

While green beans are consumed, red beans are more popular.

SAUCE CLAIRE

Vegetable & Meat Stew

(Serves 2-3)

YOU WILL NEED

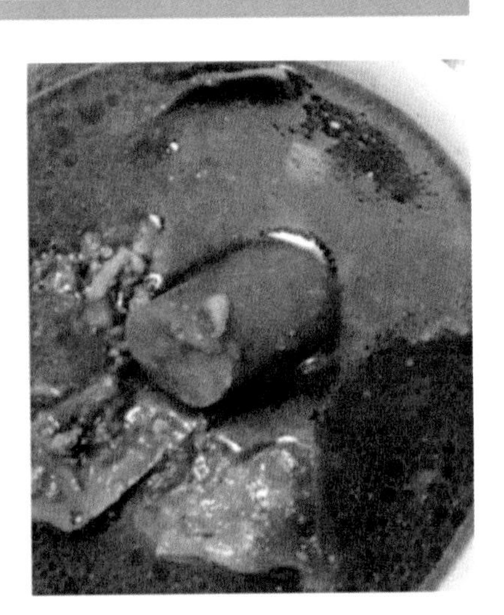

- ½ - 1 pound of pre-cooked meat (Chicken preferred.)
- 1 liter of water
- Salt and pepper to taste
- 1 large diced onion
- 4 tomatoes plus 5 tablespoons of tomato paste
- 1 small bunch of diced green onions
- 1 small bunch of chopped parsley
- 3 - 5 cloves of garlic
- 1 cup of olive oil
- ½ a cabbage cut in several pieces
- 1 cassava root
- 2 carrots cut six pieces (-/+)
- 1 purple eggplant

PROCEDURE

- In a pan, add the defrosted boiled and pre-cooked meat.
- Then, add the garlic, salt, olive oil, chopped parsley, diced onions, tomatoes and tomato paste to the pot. Stir fry until the sauce looks sautéed.
- Add the water and bring it to boil at medium heat. Once it boils, add the cabbage, carrots, and eggplant pieces.
- Taste it to see if it needs some additional seasoning such as salt and pepper. If so, add more seasoning to taste.
- Then lower the heat and let the stew cook for 15 to 30 minutes.
- When the time elapses, the stew should be a bit thicker or have less water.
- Turn off the heat. Serve and eat with some couscous, *attiéké* or rice. Refrigerate any remainder.

TOP INSIGHT

Sauce Claire is another favorite stew in Ivory Coast.

RAGOÛT DE POMME DE TERRE

Potato Stew

(Serves 4-6)

YOU WILL NEED

- 1 Ib. of potatoes
- 1 onion
- 1 clove of garlic
- 2 diced tomatoes
- Salt and black pepper to taste
- 1 teaspoon of tomato paste
- 1 teaspoon of paprika
- 1 teaspoon of cayenne pepper or ground red pepper
- Water
- Boiled and pre-cooked fresh meat. Beef meat is preferred.

PROCEDURE

- Wash and cut the potatoes in big pieces.
- In a cooking pan, add the defrosted boiled and pre-cooked fresh meat, the garlic, salt, black pepper, diced onions, tomatoes and paste to the pot of meat to be stir-fried at medium heat.
- Add 2 - 3 glasses of water and bring them to boil at medium heat.
- Add the potatoes, cayenne pepper once the stew starts boiling. Then, let the stew cook for 15 - 40 mins or until the stew thickens and the potatoes look considerably softer and cooked.
- Add salt, pepper, paprika and wait another 5 minutes to turn off the heat.
- Serve one of our favorite dish with bread if needed.

TOP INSIGHT

Ragoût is one of our family favorite dish to eat; especially during inclement weather. It was always spirit lifting and greatly enjoyed.

TÔ

Cornmeal Patty

(Serves 4-6)

YOU WILL NEED

- 1 frozen bag of fermented cornmeal paste.
- 1 - 2 liters of water

PROCEDURE

- In a large pot, mix 1 liter of water to the corn paste. Boil 1 cup of water and transfer the corn paste to it. Cook it at low heat and whip it regularly with a spatula.
- The paste will start to harden. Continue whipping it with a spatula until it completely hardens. Add ½ a cup of water to it and then, lower the heat. Let it steam for 5 - 15 minutes.
- When cooked, dip a ladle in water and then dip it back into the Tô.
- Transfer the Tô into a service plate by taking large spoonfuls of it. Continue doing this until you remove all the Tô from the cooking pot. The serving dish should be filled with small patties now.
- Eat with a stew of your liking. Sauce Kplala, Gombo with a smoked fish stew are preferred.

TOP INSIGHT

Tô is made of fine corn flour; white and yellow. It is an acquired taste. Cassava flour can also be made into this cornmeal patty and it tastes great.

In countries like Burkina Faso, shea butter and lemon are added to Tô. In Ivory Coast, the inhabitants tend to eat without these seasonings. That said, Tô with added *potasse* (edible potash) tastes better. Baking soda can be used in case you don't have *potasse*.

REAL DESSERTS

"Mangoes always remind me of summers in Ivory Coast. We had several mango trees in our backyard. So, my siblings and I used to make Mango Jam during the season."— H. Fofana

DESSERTS

TOP INSIGHT

Ivorians do not have an elaborate collection of sweet desserts like customary in other cultures. However, we remember eating fruits for desserts. We had ice cream, desserts from other cultures and crêpes on many outings but fruits were always for desserts at home and outside on many occasions. Isn't that healthier anyway?

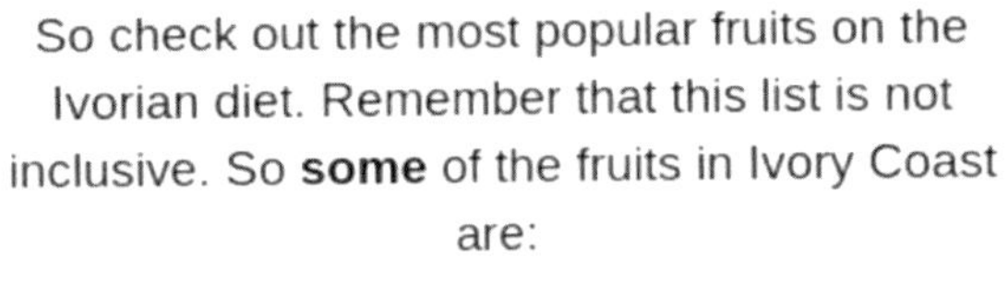

So check out the most popular fruits on the Ivorian diet. Remember that this list is not inclusive. So **some** of the fruits in Ivory Coast are:

- Mangoes. Honey mangoes are more popular.
- Pineapples, Soursop, Kiwi, Lemon, Guava, Passion Fruit, Coconut, Breadfruit, Avocado, Cocoa, Watermelon, Grapefruit, Papaya, Bananas and Baby Bananas, Apple, Cashew apple, and Côcôta (Sena Madd). The flesh of the outer-skin of Côcôta if chewed turns to chewing gum! That was fun to do during childhood.
- To continue, another fruit is Kôkôman (Badamier or Indian Almond). The seed is the '*plat de résistance!*' Break that shell to get the seed folks!
- Next, Orange péllée (Oranges are usually intricately peeled to sell).
- Mandarines, Fruits de bois (Although these fruits don't grow in Ivory Coast, the country imports them. We ate grapes, raspberries and the like on special occasions.)
- Finally, Medjool Dates. They are usually popular around Ramadan.

Interesting right! You can find many of these in Korean groceries stores or other ethnic stores. Try some of the ones you have never heard of before and enjoy the food bliss. They can be consumed in juice format as well.

Afterward

We hope you learned a tidbit of history, culture, and new recipes about Ivorian Cuisine. Turn your kitchen into an Ivorian restaurant, an *allocodrome*, a *blissidrome*, a *garbadrome*, etc. You won't regret it. If you have any questions, please don't hesitate to send us an email at info@fofkys.com . Send us your pictures too or tag us on social media! Thank you in advance!

In peace,

H. bint Youssef

Gbâkêla Chef

Fofky's Kitchen

Food & Beverages

Acknowledgments

I first want to thank Allah for inspiring me to write this cookbook. I pray it's beneficial to my family members, relatives and Ivorian students most importantly. *Aameen.*

Next, I would like to thank my family with their assistance with **Fofky's Kitchen**.

Finally, I thank my friends and supporters for their tenacity, sound and judicious advice, and support with and about the design of the book.

May Allah reward y'all. *Aameen.*

May we be neighbors in the eternal bliss. *Allahumma aameen.*

Index

T

W

Y

An Interview with an Integrative Nutrition Health Coach

This article was originally published at

Hayati Magazine on June 5th, 2018.

If you're a foodie, you know that food has a highly spiritual aspect. And our religion is about living a balanced way of life. Today, we have Zeeshan Shah, an Integrative Nutrition Health Coach, to give us some insights on her domain of expertise and what prompted her to be a Health Coach. Shah is the founder and president of **EAT.DRINK.PURE**. A wife and a mom to two boys, her passion is to educate and help women and children about all things health and wellness.

Papatia Feauxzar: *Assalamu aleikum* Zeeshan, welcome to **Hayati Magazine**. What is an Integrative Nutrition Health Coach?

Zeeshan Shah: *Wa aleikum assalam* and thank you so much for giving me the opportunity to share my passion with your readers!

To answer your question, I would like to quote my alma mater, **The Institute for Integrative Nutrition**:

"An integrative Nutrition Health Coach is a supportive mentor and wellness authority helping clients feel their best through food & lifestyle changes by tailoring individualized wellness programs to meet their clients' needs."

PF: Great! Thank you. Now, why did you decide to become one? And are there any differences between a life coach, a dietitian, a personal trainer and a nutritionist? If so, can you briefly tell us the nuances between all these terms which seem so interchangeable?

ZS: To answer your first question, I decided to become a Health Coach because I had my own health issues. I was diagnosed with **Hashimoto's.** It's an autoimmune disease. I was living overseas in Saudi Arabia at the time and as I healed myself, I became highly sensitive to the environment around me. I started noticing the lifestyle that most people had adopted in my new home.

Poor eating habits, bad sleep etiquette and a sedentary lifestyle is what has made many countries in the Middle East including Saudi Arabia among the fattest countries in the world. This didn't sit well with me at all, and I realized that I had found my calling. My community needed help, and I was going to try and provide it.

Our *deen* speaks extensively about health and wellness. We have the perfect example in our Messenger (SAW) but it seemed we, as an *ummah,* have lost our way somehow. So, I started educating people through a healthy food blog to get my message out there.

That was great for some time, but I felt I needed some credibility. So, I decided to get a certification and formally educate people.

Different Scope of Practices in the Health Field

The second part of your question deals basically with scopes of practice. With so many health professionals out there, it is *really* tough to differentiate between them but if you keep the scope of practice in mind, it is easy.

Health Coaches take a more holistic approach. Our health care system is more reactive. Therefore, Health Coaches focus on preventative care. Health Coaches **do not** diagnose or treat diseases. They work in collaboration with doctors, dietitians and other health care professionals to support the desired change that is needed for a client to reach optimal health. They fill in the gaps, if you will that doctors do not have time for.

Health Coaching is a relatively new field but you see the positions opening up in gyms and corporate settings as well as many Doctors' offices.

On the other hand, **Dietitians** and **Nutritionists** focus on treating patients through diet changes exclusively while **Health Coaches** pay attention also to the foods that nourish a client off the plate such **as spirituality, career, finances, relationships, home environment, creativity, joy and exercise.**

Life coaching and health coaching often over lap. I like to say that a Health Coach is someone who is a Life Coach but with a focus on health and nutrition.

Where Life Coaches focus mainly on a person's personal and professional goals, a Health Coach focuses on a person's health issues and is able to guide, support and hold a person accountable for reaching their specific health related goals.

As far as **Personal Trainers** are concerned, they help people with their fitness goals. They do offer advice on nutrition but the focus is mainly on the client's fitness.

PF: Thank you for the thorough description of these terms! To continue, how do you help your clients and the *ummah*?

ZS: I help my clients by educating them about health and wellness through 1:1 coaching. I also help my clients chart out customized plans to achieve their specific health goals. These sessions can be in person, through the phone or video calls. I am working on an online jumpstart program to help those who are unable to take out the time for the 1:1 sessions.

I also conduct workshops and cooking demonstrations at my local mosque and in private homes. I did several talks on achieving a healthier Ramadan prior to the month and recently published an eBook which is free to the public to educate them on the benefits of fasting as well as providing tips and recipes on making it a healthy and productive one.

PF: Thanks for the eBook. *Alhamdullilah,* I was fortunate enough to work with you, and it tremendously helped. I mean my life was chaotic, and it affected every aspect of me from spirituality to career, health, financial, creativity, etc. How about yourself? Did you have to work with a coach in your life and was it beneficial?

ZS: I was unfortunately not able to find a Health Coach when I was going through my own struggles. As I mentioned earlier, I was overseas at the time, and I didn't even know such a professional existed. I did go to several Doctors. However, none of them told me that I needed to make any food or lifestyle changes. I wish I had a Health Coach though because I kept falling off track as I was learning about my condition and what would have taken me a few months to heal, took me much longer.

I became depressed for a while too because I had eliminated many foods from my diet and had no game plan. I am grateful to Allah (SWT) who guided me to two people; Lee Holmes, a Health Coach and Dr.Mark Hyman, a functional medicine Doctor. I bought Lee's book "Heal your Gut" which made all the difference. I also started following Dr. Mark Hyman's blog where he posts about getting to the root cause of disease. You can read more about my journey on my blog http://www.eatdrinkpure.com/blog/.

PF: *Masha'Allah alhamdullilah*. I'm happy you find your way somehow amidst the storm. Now, I love *halal* comfort food. It's not always healthy but it feeds my soul *laughs*. Is there anything wrong with that? In other words, what would you say a good balance is?

ZS: There is absolutely nothing wrong with eating foods that feed your soul, and if it is *halal,* then you have nothing to worry about because *halal* means pure and lawful :)!I always say, eat well 80-90% of the time so you can splurge the rest of the time. The problem starts when we eat the bad stuff almost all of the time. Also, it is important to know what makes your body thrive. We are *individual beings;* what's one person's food may be another person's poison.

PF: *Alhamdullilah,* good to know! Last question. What is the most common issue you encounter in your field?

ZS: I have a lot of people asking me about healthy eating. What and how they should eat. Weight loss also comes up more than other issues. The beauty is that if you eat clean, you are almost always guaranteed weigh loss :). I also see a lot of moms interested in getting their kids to eat right. This is such a wonderful shift. We are more aware as moms and are keen to take steps in the right direction. Often, it is better received when others tell you to eat right with solid scientific backing rather than your own mom right?

PF: Right! Well, the team at **Hayati Magazine** wishes you *mubarak* success enlightening the *ummah* and also gifting your knowledge for the sake of Allah. It was an immense honor and pleasure to interview you Zeeshan. We sincerely thank you for being with us. Please give us your social media links so that our readers can learn about you and your works *insha'Allah*. In peace.

ZS: Oh the pleasure and honor was all mine! Thank you for this opportunity. I hope that my work benefits the *ummah* and makes us look at what we eat and treat food as medicine and go back to the sage advice offered by the Quran and the Sunnah!

Read more about Zeeshan Shah at **www.eatdrinkpure.com**.

Made in the USA
Middletown, DE
18 December 2023